EDITOR: Maryanne Blacker

FOOD EDITOR: Pamela Clark

DESIGN DIRECTOR: Neil Carlyle

■ ■ ■

DESIGNER: Robbylee Phelan

■ ■ ■

ASSISTANT FOOD EDITOR:
Barbara Northwood

ASSOCIATE FOOD EDITOR: Enid Morrison

HOME ECONOMISTS: Lucy Clayton,
Wendy Berecry, Jo-anne Power,
Jane Cleary, Sue Hipwell

EDITORIAL ASSISTANT: Denise Prentice

KITCHEN ASSISTANT: Amy Wong

■ ■ ■

PHOTOGRAPHER: Ashley Mackevicius

FOOD STYLIST: Jacqui Hing

■ ■ ■

HOME LIBRARY STAFF:

ASSISTANT EDITOR: Judy Newman

DESIGNER: Paula Wooller

SECRETARY: Sanchia Roth

■ ■ ■

PUBLISHER: Richard Walsh

DEPUTY PUBLISHER: Graham Lawrence

ASSOCIATE PUBLISHER Bob Neil

■ ■ ■

Produced by The Australian Women's Weekly
Home Library
Typeset by Photoset Computer Service Pty Ltd,
and Letter Perfect, Sydney. Printed by Dai Nippon Co., Ltd in
Japan. Published by Australian Consolidated Press,
54 Park Street Sydney. Distributed by Network Distribution
Company, 54 Park Street Sydney. Distributed in the U.K. by
Australian Consolidated Press (UK)Ltd (0604) 760 456.
Distributed in Canada by Whitecap Books Ltd
(604) 980 9852. Distributed in South Africa by Intermag
(011) 493 3200. Distributed in New Zealand by Netlink
Distribution Company, 302 7616

■ ■ ■

Light and Luscious Summertime Cookbook
Includes index
ISBN 0 949892 74 0.

1.Cookery. (Series: Australian Women's
Weekly Home Library)
641.5'64.

■ ■ ■

© A C P 1991 (Reprint)
This publication is copyright. No part of it may be reproduced
or transmitted in any form without the written permission of
the publishers.

■ ■ ■

COVER: Clockwise from front left: Cracked Wheat and
Minted Lamb Salad, Peppered King Prawns, Marinated Cold
Fish Salad, Hot Stir-Fried Vegetable Salad
with Orange Dressing, Bacon and Pine Nut Salad,
Orange and Onion Salad.
BACK COVER: Strawberry and Passionfruit
Ice-Cream Victoria.
OPPOSITE: Clockwise from top: Tiered stand from top: Mini
Apricot Florentines, Nutty Caramel Triangles, Fruit Mince
and Apple Tartlets, Moist Coconut Almond Cake, Honey
Roll, Liqueur Double Indulgence, Chocolate Mousse, Mini
Apple Tart Tatin and Chocolate Rainbow Meringues,
Hazelnut Meringue Cake with Kahlua Cream.

Light & Luscious Summertime Cookbook

The emphasis in our Summertime Cookbook is on both the light and the luscious, with an eye to food that is nutritious as well as visually exciting and satisfying. Seafood is important and you'll find that salads have been given new meaning. Pizzas, pasta, chicken and meat dishes are presented in a variety of ways to provide many menu options. Salt is rarely used in our recipes; remember to allow for the saltiness of stock cubes, canned and packaged goods when seasoning food. We have included advice on preparing food ahead of serving time, with freezing and microwave advice where applicable.

Pamela Clark

FOOD EDITOR

BRITISH &NORTH AMERICAN READERS: Please note that conversion charts for cup
and spoon measurements and oven temperatures are on page 126.

CONTENTS

FRESH STARTS

We give you salads that combine an adventurous profusion of ingredients, creating warm, hot or cold dishes which are light and delicious. All are suitable for getting a meal off to a great start and many could be served as main courses.

LOBSTER MEDALLION SALAD WITH HONEY CHILLI SAUCE

This recipe is also delicious if green prawns are substituted for lobster; you will need three large green prawns per person. We used a hot Asian chilli sauce in this recipe.

3 green lobster tails
⅓ cup honey
2 teaspoons chilli sauce
⅔ cup dry white wine
1 teaspoon grated fresh ginger
2 carrots
2 zucchini
1 teaspoon cornflour
2 teaspoons water
1 small fresh red chilli, chopped

Remove lobster flesh from shells, cut flesh into 1cm slices. Combine honey, chilli sauce, wine and ginger, pour half the mixture into large shallow pan (reserve remaining mixture for sauce). Add lobster to pan, bring to the boil, cover, reduce heat, simmer for about 4 minutes or until the lobster is tender; drain. Or you can microwave lobster on MEDIUM HIGH for about 5 minutes.

Cut carrots and zucchini into thin strips about 5cm long. Boil, steam or microwave carrot strips until tender; drain, rinse under cold water. Combine carrots and zucchini in bowl, cover, refrigerate 1 hour. Place lobster and carrot mixture onto serving plates. Place remaining honey mixture into pan, stir in blended cornflour and water, stir constantly over heat until mixture boils and thickens; add chilli. Serve immediately over cold lobster.

Serves 6.

BELOW: Lobster Medallion Salad with Honey Chilli Sauce.

PECAN AND ENDIVE SALAD WITH GARLIC DRESSING

1 cup (100g) pecan nuts
3 cups chopped endive
1 bunch radishes, sliced
2 tablespoons chopped parsley
4 green shallots, chopped
GARLIC DRESSING
¼ cup oil
1½ tablespoons red wine vinegar
1 clove garlic, crushed

Toast pecans on oven tray in moderate oven for about 5 minutes. Combine endive, radishes, parsley, shallots, pecans and Dressing; toss well.

Garlic Dressing: Combine all ingredients in jar; shake well.

Serves 4.

SWEET POTATO SALAD WITH GINGER ORANGE DRESSING

2 tablespoons oil
2 large sweet potatoes, sliced
2 sticks celery, chopped
4 green shallots, finely chopped
½ small red cabbage, finely shredded
GINGER ORANGE DRESSING
¼ cup orange juice
1 teaspoon grated fresh ginger
2 teaspoons honey
¼ teaspoon ground cumin

Heat oil in large pan, add sweet potatoes, cook until potatoes are just tender; drain on absorbent paper. Combine celery and shallots with Dressing. Place cabbage onto serving plates, top with potatoes, then celery mixture.

Ginger Orange Dressing: Combine all ingredients in jar; shake well.

Serves 6.

FRESH BEETROOT AND ARTICHOKE SALAD WITH WALNUT DRESSING

Canned drained whole baby beetroot can be used instead of fresh beetroot in this recipe.

1 bunch (about 4) beetroot
400g can artichoke hearts, drained
1 avocado, chopped
⅓ cup walnut halves
4 green shallots, finely chopped
1 cup alfalfa sprouts
WALNUT DRESSING
¼ cup oil
2 tablespoons walnut oil
2 tablespoons white wine vinegar
1 teaspoon French mustard
1 clove garlic, crushed

Top and tail beetroot, boil, steam or microwave until tender. Drain beetroot, cool, peel by pushing the skin away with fingers, cut beetroot into quarters.

Combine the beetroot, artichoke hearts, avocado, walnuts and shallots in bowl, add Dressing. Place sprouts on serving plates, top with beetroot mixture; serve immediately.

Walnut Dressing: Combine all ingredients in jar; shake well.

Serves 4.

BELOW: Back: Pecan and Endive Salad with Garlic Dressing; centre: Sweet Potato Salad with Ginger Orange Dressing; front: Fresh Beetroot and Artichoke Salad with Walnut Dressing.
RIGHT: From top: Crab and Salmon Salad; Creamy Scallop and Rice Salad; Marinated Squid and Lime Salad.

CRAB AND SALMON SALAD

4 small cooked crabs
1½ cups alfalfa sprouts
4 green shallots, chopped
440g can red salmon, drained
DRESSING
½ cup mayonnaise
1 tablespoon chopped gherkin
1 tablespoon chopped parsley
2 green shallots, chopped

Remove triangular flap on underside of crabs, insert knife through slit where flap has been removed. Lever shell away from body, wash shell. Remove grey fibrous tissue from body, flake crab flesh. To remove flesh from claws and legs, break shells with hammer or mallet. Combine the crab flesh with sprouts, shallots and salmon which has been broken into chunks. Spoon into crab shells, top with Dressing.
Dressing: Combine all ingredients well.
　Serves 4.

CREAMY SCALLOP AND RICE SALAD

750g scallops
½ cup dry white wine
1 cup water
1 onion, finely chopped
½ cup wild rice
½ cup brown rice
1 cup watercress leaves
4 green shallots, chopped
2 tablespoons chopped parsley
DRESSING
⅓ cup sour cream
2 tablespoons mayonnaise
2 tablespoons French dressing

Trim scallops. Combine wine, water and onion in pan, bring to the boil, boil 2 minutes, add scallops to pan. Return water to the boil, remove from heat (scallops will finish cooking while cooling); drain when cold.

　Add wild and brown rice gradually to large pan of rapidly boiling water, boil constantly, uncovered, for about 30 minutes or until rice is just tender; drain, cool. Combine scallops, rice, watercress and shallots, top with Dressing; sprinkle with parsley.
Dressing: Combine all ingredients well.
　Serves 6.

MARINATED SQUID AND LIME SALAD

500g squid hoods
2 tablespoons lime juice
4 green shallots, chopped
1 tablespoon chopped parsley
1 teaspoon chopped fresh basil
1 small red pepper, chopped
mignonette lettuce

Cut squid into rings, drop rings into pan of boiling water, boil for about 30 seconds, or until squid is opaque; drain, rinse under cold water. Combine squid with lime juice, shallots, parsley, basil and pepper; cover, refrigerate 2 hours or overnight. Place lettuce leaves on serving plates, top with squid mixture.
　Serves 4.

TOMATO AND CHEESE SALAD WITH BASIL VINAIGRETTE

Bocconcini are small fresh mozzarella cheeses sold loose in delicatessens.

6 tomatoes, peeled
mignonette lettuce
2 bocconcini, sliced
2 green shallots, finely chopped
2 tablespoons grated parmesan
  cheese
BASIL VINAIGRETTE
½ cup olive oil
¼ cup red wine vinegar
1 tablespoon chopped fresh basil
1 clove garlic, crushed
1 teaspoon sugar

BELOW: Clockwise from left: Tomato and Cheese Salad with Basil Vinaigrette; Bacon and Pine Nut Salad; Red Pasta Salad with Italian Dressing.

FRUITY COTTAGE CHEESE SALAD WITH ORANGE DRESSING

2 oranges
1 stick celery
400g cottage cheese
½ teaspoon grated orange rind
mignonette lettuce
1 apple, thinly sliced
ORANGE DRESSING
½ cup oil
¼ cup red wine vinegar
¼ cup orange juice
2 teaspoons sugar
¼ teaspoon ground basil
¼ teaspoon ground tarragon

Segment oranges by peeling oranges thickly and removing all white pith. Cut down beside each segment to release them from the joining membranes.

Cut celery into thin strips about 5cm long. Combine cheese with orange rind and half the orange segments in a bowl. Place lettuce onto serving plates, top with cheese mixture. Serve with remaining oranges, celery and apple; top with Dressing.
Orange Dressing: Combine all ingredients in jar; shake well.

Serves 4.

ROQUEFORT AND WALNUT SALAD WITH MUSTARD DRESSING

100g roquefort cheese
1 cup (100g) walnut pieces
2 apples, sliced
1 radicchio lettuce
1 bunch watercress
MUSTARD DRESSING
2 tablespoons seeded mustard
2 tablespoons white wine vinegar
1 tablespoon dry white wine
½ cup oil

Crumble cheese into bowl, add walnuts, apples and half the Dressing, mix gently. Place lettuce and watercress on serving plates, top with remaining Dressing, then cheese mixture.
Mustard Dressing: Combine all ingredients in jar; shake well.

Serves 6.

ABOVE: Back: Fruity Cottage Cheese Salad with Orange Dressing; front: Roquefort and Walnut Salad with Mustard Dressing.

Slice tomatoes, cut in half. Place lettuce on serving plates, top with tomato and bocconcini, sprinkle with shallots and parmesan cheese. Serve topped with Vinaigrette.

Basil Vinaigrette: Combine all ingredients in jar; shake well.

Serves 6.

RED PASTA SALAD WITH ITALIAN DRESSING

Red fettucine is usually tomato- or red pepper-flavored pasta and is readily available from delicatessens or stores which stock fresh pasta. Cooking time for pasta is between three and 15 minutes depending on the type used. Fresh pasta takes the least time to cook and dried packaged pasta takes the longest. Any shape or any colored pasta can be used.

500g red fettucine
125g snow peas
125g prosciutto, chopped
230g can sliced water chestnuts, drained
1 small red pepper, chopped
ITALIAN DRESSING
½ cup olive oil
¼ cup lemon juice
1 clove garlic, crushed
6 pitted black olives, sliced

Add pasta to large pan of rapidly boiling water; boil rapidly, uncovered, until just tender; drain. Combine pasta with Dressing in bowl. Top and tail snow peas. Boil, steam or microwave snow peas until just tender; drain, place into a bowl of iced water; drain, add snow peas to pasta with prosciutto, water chestnuts and pepper.

Italian Dressing: Combine all ingredients in jar; shake well.

Serves 6.

BACON AND PINE NUT SALAD

The no-oil dressing is a commercial, bottled low-kilojoule dressing.

½ cup pine nuts
1 bunch endive, chopped
1 cos lettuce
6 green shallots, chopped
6 bacon rashers, chopped
2 teaspoons brown sugar
1 cup no-oil French dressing

Toast pine nuts on oven tray in moderate oven for about 5 minutes, cool. Combine endive, roughly torn cos lettuce, pine nuts and shallots in bowl. Cook bacon in pan until crisp, add sugar and dressing, bring to the boil. Serve the hot dressing over salad; serve immediately.

Serves 6.

ROAST QUAIL AND SESAME SALAD

6 quail
2 carrots
6 green shallots
2 tablespoons sesame seeds
¼ red cabbage, shredded
MARINADE
½ cup oil
¼ cup orange juice
2 tablespoons honey
1 tablespoon sesame oil
1 clove garlic, crushed
DRESSING
2 tablespoons orange juice
2 tablespoons dry white wine
2 teaspoons sesame oil
2 teaspoons grated fresh ginger

Combine quail with Marinade, cover, stand 2 hours or refrigerate overnight. Place quail on rack over baking dish, bake in moderate oven 30 minutes or until quail are tender. Baste quail occasionally with Marinade during cooking.

Cut carrots and shallots into thin strips about 5cm long. Place sesame seeds in pan, stir constantly over heat until golden brown, remove from pan immediately; cool.

Cut quail into quarters. Toss cabbage, carrots and shallots with Dressing. Place on serving plates, top with quail, sprinkle with sesame seeds.
Marinade: Combine all ingredients.
Dressing: Combine all ingredients in jar; shake well.
Serves 6.

FRESH ASPARAGUS WITH WARM PEPPERCORN SAUCE

250g asparagus
mignonette lettuce
WARM PEPPERCORN SAUCE
15g butter
1 small onion, finely chopped
1 tablespoon canned green
    peppercorns, drained
2 tablespoons brandy
⅓ cup sour cream

Trim asparagus, boil, steam or microwave until just tender; drain, place into iced water; drain. Place lettuce and asparagus onto plates, top with Sauce.
Warm Peppercorn Sauce: Melt butter in pan, add onion, saute 1 minute; add crushed peppercorns, saute 2 minutes. (Or microwave on HIGH 3 minutes). Remove from heat, stir in brandy and cream. Reheat without boiling; serve immediately.
Serves 4.

WARM SALAD OF BRAINS AND ARTICHOKES

Bottled artichokes in oil can be bought at delicatessens.

6 sets lamb brains
6 slices white bread
60g butter, melted
¾ cup dry white wine
¼ cup lemon juice
90g cold butter
2 tablespoons chopped parsley
1 bunch watercress
8 bottled artichokes, quartered

Place brains in bowl, cover with water, stand 1 hour; drain, peel away membrane. Place brains in pan, cover brains with cold water, bring to the boil, reduce heat, simmer, uncovered, 2 minutes; drain. Cut a 7cm round from each slice of bread, brush with melted butter, place on oven tray, toast in moderate oven for about 10 minutes.

Combine wine and lemon juice in pan, bring to the boil, reduce heat, add brains, simmer, uncovered, 2 minutes on each side. Remove brains from pan, keep warm. Bring the stock to the boil, reduce heat, simmer, uncovered, until mixture is reduced by half, remove from heat, gradually whisk in small blocks of cold butter until mixture is slightly thickened; stir in the chopped parsley. Place watercress and artichokes on serving plates, top with bread and brains, cover with hot sauce; serve immediately.
Serves 6.

WARM SALAD OF SWEETBREADS WITH LEMON MUSTARD DRESSING

500g sweetbreads
plain flour
60g butter
2 leeks
2 zucchini
1 carrot
1 bunch English spinach
1 tablespoon oil
LEMON MUSTARD DRESSING
2 tablespoons seeded mustard
1 tablespoon lemon juice
1 tablespoon dry white wine
¼ cup oil

Soak sweetbreads in cold water for 1 hour; drain, remove any fat. Place sweetbreads in pan, cover with cold water. Bring to the boil, reduce heat, simmer, uncovered, 2 minutes; drain. Peel membrane from sweetbreads, cut into 1cm slices, toss in flour. Melt butter in pan, add sweetbreads, cook 2 minutes or until golden brown, turning occasionally; keep warm.

Cut leeks, zucchini and carrot into thin strips about 5cm long, add to pan of boiling water, boil 1 minute; drain, rinse under cold water. Remove stems from spinach, heat oil in pan, add spinach, cook, stirring, 2 minutes. Place spinach onto plates, top with vegetables, sweetbreads and Dressing.
Lemon Mustard Dressing: Combine all ingredients in jar; shake well.
Serves 6.

SALMON AND CRAB MOUSSE WITH FRESH DILL DRESSING

220g can red salmon, drained
220g can crab, drained
⅔ cup thickened cream
½ cup thousand island dressing
¼ cup chopped pickled onions
1 teaspoon dry mustard
1 tablespoon gelatine
2 tablespoons water
FRESH DILL DRESSING
½ cup sour cream
2 tablespoons French dressing
1 tablespoon chopped fresh dill

Blend or process salmon, crab, cream, dressing, onions and mustard until smooth. Sprinkle gelatine over water, dissolve over hot water, cool, stir into salmon mixture. Pour mixture into 6 individual serving dishes (½ cup capacity), refrigerate several hours or until set. Turn onto serving plates, serve with Dressing.

Fresh Dill Dressing: Combine all ingredients thoroughly.
Serves 6.

LEFT: Salmon and Crab Mousse with Fresh Dill Dressing.

WILD RICE AND PRAWN SALAD
500g cooked prawns
1 litre (4 cups) chicken stock
½ cup wild rice
2 large spinach leaves, shredded
125g baby mushrooms, sliced
4 green shallots, chopped
1 red pepper, sliced
DRESSING
⅓ cup olive oil
2 tablespoons lemon juice
1 clove garlic, crushed

Bring stock to the boil in pan, add rice, simmer, uncovered, for about 30 minutes or until rice is tender; drain.

Shell and devein prawns. Combine rice with prawns, spinach, mushrooms, shallots and pepper. Add Dressing, toss well, cover, refrigerate 2 hours before serving.

Dressing: Combine all ingredients.
Serves 4.

SCALLOP AND CUCUMBER SALAD WITH LIME CORIANDER DRESSING
500g scallops
4 long cucumbers, peeled, sliced
2 tomatoes, peeled, chopped
1 onion, chopped
LIME CORIANDER DRESSING
¼ cup lime juice
¼ cup dry white wine
1 teaspoon sugar
¼ cup oil
1 tablespoon chopped fresh coriander

Trim scallops, combine with cucumbers, tomatoes and onion. Add hot Dressing, cover, marinate overnight in refrigerator before serving.

Lime Coriander Dressing: Combine lime juice, wine and sugar in pan, bring to the boil, remove from heat. Whisk in oil and coriander, use immediately.
Serves 6.

PRAWN AND AVOCADO SALAD
1kg cooked king prawns
mignonette lettuce
2 avocados, sliced
2 tablespoons chopped chives
MAYONNAISE
1 cup mayonnaise
2 tablespoons lemon juice
1 small fresh red chilli, finely chopped
1 clove garlic, crushed
few drops tabasco sauce

Shell and devein prawns. Place lettuce on serving plates, top with prawns and avocados, then Mayonnaise. Sprinkle with the chives.

Mayonnaise: Combine all ingredients.
Serves 6.

LEFT: From top: Wild Rice and Prawn Salad; Scallop and Cucumber Salad with Lime Coriander Dressing; Prawn and Avocado Salad.

MAIN ATTRACTIONS

For salads of substance that can stand on their own as main courses, we've combined seafood, poultry and meat with an abundant array of salad vegetables and complemented their flavors with out-of-the-ordinary dressings and mayonnaises.

KING PRAWN AND MANGO SALAD WITH COCONUT DRESSING

You will need to boil about two-thirds cup rice for this recipe.

1kg cooked king prawns
lettuce
2 cups cooked rice
2 mangoes, sliced
1 avocado, sliced
COCONUT DRESSING
½ cup coconut cream
1 teaspoon grated fresh ginger
2 tablespoons lemon juice
2 teaspoons sugar
½ teaspoon curry powder
¼ teaspoon turmeric

Shell prawns, leave tails intact; devein prawns. Place lettuce and rice onto serving plates, top with prawns, mangoes and avocado, then the Dressing.
Coconut Dressing: Place all ingredients in jar; shake well.
   Serves 4.

TROPICAL FRUIT, PRAWN AND PASTA SALAD

1½kg cooked prawns
200g pasta
1 mango
1 pawpaw
440g can unsweetened pineapple pieces, drained
300g can mandarin segments, drained
3 green shallots, sliced
DRESSING
½ cup cream
2 tablespoons coconut cream
1 tablespoon mayonnaise
1 tablespoon grated fresh ginger
1 tablespoon lime juice

Add pasta to large pan of boiling water, boil rapidly, uncovered, for about 10 minutes or until tender; drain, cool.
   Shell and devein prawns. Peel mango and pawpaw and chop into chunks. Combine prawns, mango, pawpaw, pineapple and mandarins with Dressing in bowl. Combine pasta and shallots, place on serving plates; top with salad mixture.
Dressing: Combine all ingredients thoroughly.
   Serves 6.

LEFT: Back: King Prawn and Mango Salad with Coconut Dressing; front: Tropical Fruit, Prawn and Pasta Salad.

CHICKEN, WATERCRESS AND SMOKED SALMON SALAD

6 chicken breast fillets
5 slices smoked salmon, chopped
2 sticks celery, sliced
4 gherkins, chopped
2 teaspoons capers, chopped
1 bunch watercress
DRESSING
¼ cup olive oil
¼ cup lemon juice
1 egg yolk
1 teaspoon French mustard
1 clove garlic, crushed

Poach chicken, covered, in a pan of simmering water for about 10 minutes or until tender; remove from pan, cool, cut chicken into strips.

Combine chicken with salmon, celery, gherkins, capers and watercress sprigs in bowl with Dressing; refrigerate 1 hour before serving.

Dressing: Whisk all the ingredients together in bowl.

Serves 4.

CREAMY CHICKEN SALAD WITH MANGO DRESSING

6 chicken breast fillets
1 cup chicken stock
¾ cup rice
2 mangoes
3 green shallots, chopped
2 tablespoons French dressing
MANGO DRESSING
1 mango
½ cup cream
¼ cup thousand island dressing
1 tablespoon mango chutney
1 tablespoon chopped mint

Place chicken stock in pan, add chicken, cover, bring to the boil, reduce heat, simmer 10 minutes or until chicken is tender; drain, cool. Add rice gradually to a large pan of boiling water, boil rapidly, uncovered, for about 10 minutes or until rice is tender; drain, cool.

Cut mango into thin strips, combine with rice, shallots and dressing in bowl; place onto plates, top with chicken and Mango Dressing.

Mango Dressing: Blend or process all ingredients until smooth.

Serves 6.

SMOKED CHICKEN SALAD WITH VERMOUTH MAYONNAISE

1kg smoked chicken
2 carrots
3 small zucchini
5 green shallots
VERMOUTH MAYONNAISE
3 egg yolks
1 teaspoon French mustard
2 teaspoons tarragon vinegar
½ cup oil
¼ cup dry vermouth

Cut chicken, carrots, zucchini and shallots into thin strips, place into bowl, mix in Mayonnaise, cover; stand 1 hour before serving.

Vermouth Mayonnaise: Blend or process egg yolks, mustard and vinegar, until smooth, add oil gradually in a thin stream while motor is operating; mix in the vermouth.

Serves 4.

BELOW: Clockwise from top: Hot Fettucine Salad with Tomato Dressing; Chicken and Almond Salad with Creamy Chive Dressing; Smoked Chicken Salad with Vermouth Mayonnaise; Creamy Chicken Salad with Mango Dressing; Chicken, Watercress and Smoked Salmon Salad.

CHICKEN AND ALMOND SALAD WITH CREAMY CHIVE DRESSING

6 chicken breast fillets
⅓ cup blanched almonds
1 apple, chopped
2 sticks celery, sliced
2 tablespoons sultanas
CREAMY CHIVE DRESSING
½ cup mayonnaise
½ cup sour cream
1 tablespoon lemon juice
2 tablespoons chopped chives

Poach chicken, covered, in pan of simmering water for about 10 minutes or until just tender; remove from pan, cool. Toast almonds on oven tray in moderate oven for about 5 minutes.

Cut chicken into strips, combine in bowl with Dressing, almonds, apple, celery and sultanas; refrigerate 1 hour before serving.

Creamy Chive Dressing: Combine all ingredients in bowl; mix well.

Serves 6.

HOT FETTUCINE SALAD WITH TOMATO DRESSING

We used a mixture of plain, spinach and tomato-flavored fettucine in this recipe. Cooking time differs for fresh and dried pasta; usually between three and 15 minutes.

4 chicken breast fillets, sliced
750g fettucine
30g butter
½ cup pine nuts
432g can red kidney beans, drained
400g can artichoke hearts, drained
250g baby mushrooms, sliced
TOMATO DRESSING
2 tablespoons oil
2 onions, chopped
4 large tomatoes, chopped
1 teaspoon dried basil leaves
2 teaspoons brown sugar
1 tablespoon tomato paste

Cook fettucine in a large pan of boiling water until just tender; drain. Melt butter in pan, add pine nuts, saute until lightly browned; drain. Add chicken to pan, saute until lightly browned all over. Add beans, artichokes and mushrooms, stir until hot, mix in fettucine. Serve hot with hot Dressing.

Tomato Dressing: Heat oil in pan, add onions, saute until onions are soft. Add tomatoes, basil, sugar and tomato paste. Bring to the boil, reduce heat, simmer uncovered 10 minutes or until tomatoes are pulpy and liquid is reduced by half. Blend or process until smooth, strain, reheat if necessary.

Serves 6.

BEEF AND PASTA SALAD WITH PESTO DRESSING

1½ kg beef eye fillet (in one piece)
30g butter
1 tablespoon oil
250g pasta
¾ cup chopped black olives
2 tomatoes, peeled, chopped
8 canned artichokes, quartered
2 tablespoons grated parmesan cheese
PESTO DRESSING
2 cups fresh basil leaves
¼ cup oil
2 cloves garlic, crushed
¼ cup grated parmesan cheese
2 tablespoons pine nuts

Remove any excess fat from beef. Heat butter and oil in pan, add beef, cook over high heat, turning often, until lightly browned all over. Place on rack over baking dish, brush with about ¼ cup of the Dressing. Bake in moderately hot oven 20 minutes or until tender. Cook pasta in boiling water for about 10 minutes or until just tender; drain. Combine pasta, olives, tomatoes, artichokes and the remaining Dressing in bowl; mix well. Place pasta mixture onto serving plates, top with sliced beef, sprinkle with cheese.

Pesto Dressing: Blend or process all ingredients until smooth.

Serves 6.

ABOVE: Beef and Pasta Salad with Pesto Dressing.

13

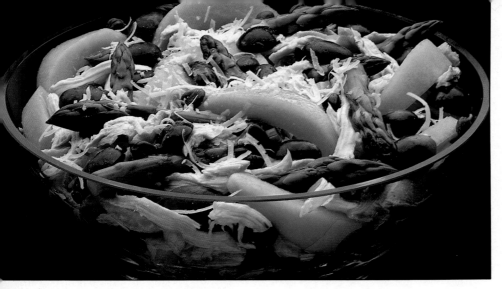

DELI SALAD WITH PARSLEY DRESSING
375g pasta
125g sliced pastrami
250g sliced smoked turkey
125g stuffed olives
250g punnet cherry tomatoes
250g smoked cheese, cubed
PARSLEY DRESSING
2 tablespoons chopped parsley
⅓ cup oil
2 tablespoons red wine vinegar
½ teaspoon dried basil leaves

Add pasta to large pan of rapidly boiling water, boil uncovered for about 10 minutes or until just tender; drain. Cut pastrami and turkey into strips, combine with pasta, olives, tomatoes, cheese and Dressing.

Parsley Dressing: Combine all ingredients in jar; shake well.

Serves 6.

SMOKED TURKEY AND KIWI FRUIT WITH PEPPERCORN DRESSING
750g smoked turkey breast
4 oranges
3 kiwi fruit, sliced
PEPPERCORN DRESSING
¼ cup orange juice
2 tablespoons oil
1 teaspoon grated fresh ginger
1 tablespoon canned green
    peppercorns, drained
2 teaspoons honey

Segment oranges by peeling thickly and cutting down between adjoining membranes to release the segments. Cut turkey into thin strips, place in bowl; mix in orange segments, kiwi fruit and Dressing.

Peppercorn Dressing: Place all ingredients in jar; shake well.

Serves 6.

FRANKFURT, DILL PICKLE AND POTATO SALAD
500g frankfurts
1kg potatoes, diced
6 hard-boiled eggs, chopped
1 green pepper, chopped
1 cup chopped dill pickles
DRESSING
1 small onion, finely chopped
300g carton sour cream
2 tablespoons horseradish cream
2 tablespoons mayonnaise

Score frankfurts diagonally. Boil, steam or microwave potatoes until just tender; drain, cool.

Combine potatoes, eggs, pepper, pickles and Dressing in bowl, place on serving plates. Grill frankfurts for about 10 minutes or until heated through; serve hot over potato mixture.

Dressing: Combine all ingredients in bowl; mix well.

Serves 6.

SALAD OF CHICKEN AND MELON
6 chicken breast fillets
1 rockmelon
250g black grapes
250g bunch asparagus
1 cup chicken stock
½ cup dry white wine
1 clove garlic, crushed
2 tablespoons capers
2 tablespoons coarsely grated
    parmesan cheese
DRESSING
¼ cup lemon juice
¼ cup oil
¼ cup dry white wine
1 clove garlic, crushed

Cut rockmelon into chunks, halve and seed grapes. Trim asparagus, boil, steam or microwave until just tender; drain, cut into 5cm lengths. Combine stock, wine and garlic in large pan; add chicken, bring to the boil, reduce heat, simmer for about 5 minutes on each side, or until chicken is tender. Drain chicken, cool; shred finely.

Combine chicken, melon, grapes, asparagus and capers with Dressing. Serve sprinkled with cheese.

Dressing: Combine all ingredients in jar; shake well.

Serves 6.

FRIED SAUSAGES, ONION AND PASTA SALAD
375g chipolata sausages
90g butter
2 onions, sliced
1kg pumpkin
500g pasta
DRESSING
½ cup sour cream
2 tablespoons French dressing
2 tablespoons tomato sauce

*ABOVE: Salad of Chicken and Melon.
RIGHT: Clockwise from top: Deli Salad with Parsley Dressing; Fried Sausages, Onion and Pasta Salad; Marinated Beef Salad; Smoked Turkey and Kiwi Fruit with Peppercorn Dressing; Frankfurt, Dill Pickle and Potato Salad.*

Melt 30g of the butter in pan, add sausages, fry until cooked through; drain; cut sausages in half. Melt remaining butter in pan, add onions, fry until lightly browned, remove from pan. Add sausages, fry until crisp.

Cut pumpkin into 5cm strips, boil or steam until just tender; drain, rinse under cold water. Add pasta to pan of boiling water, boil about 10 minutes or until tender; drain, cool. Combine sausages with onions, pumpkin, pasta and Dressing.

Dressing: Combine all ingredients.

Serves 4.

MARINATED BEEF SALAD

Quick Cook Wheat is available at supermarkets and is a delicious alternative to rice or pasta. Follow directions for cooking on the packet. Seasoned Wheat can be used instead; it has additional flavoring.

1kg beef eye fillet (in one piece)
¼ cup cream
¾ cup Quick Cook Wheat
MARINADE
2 tablespoons French mustard
2 tablespoons seeded mustard
2 tablespoons brown sugar
2 tablespoons tomato sauce
1 tablespoon Worcestershire sauce
1 tablespoon red wine vinegar
1 tablespoon oil
1 clove garlic, crushed

Combine beef and Marinade ingredients in bowl; cover, stand several hours or refrigerate overnight.

Place beef in baking dish, reserve remaining Marinade. Cook beef in moderate oven 20 to 30 minutes or until beef is tender and done as desired. Cool, refrigerate before slicing thinly. Place remaining Marinade in pan, bring to the boil, remove from heat, stir in cream; reheat. Place Wheat on serving plates, top with sliced beef, then cream sauce.

Marinade: Combine all ingredients in bowl; mix well.

Serves 6.

RED SALMON AND BASIL SALAD

2 x 440g cans red salmon, drained
¼ cup lemon juice
4 cucumbers, sliced
250g punnet cherry tomatoes, halved
6 radishes, sliced
1 lettuce
2 tablespoons fresh basil leaves
DRESSING
⅓ cup oil
2 tablespoons lemon juice
1 clove garlic, crushed

Remove skin and bones from salmon. Place salmon in bowl with lemon juice, cucumbers, tomatoes, radishes and basil; mix in Dressing. Place lettuce on plates; top with salmon mixture.

Dressing: Combine all ingredients in jar; shake well.

Serves 6.

TUNA AND RICE SALAD WITH SWEET CURRY DRESSING

425g can tuna, drained
1 cup brown rice
1 apple, chopped
⅓ cup chopped raisins
3 green shallots, chopped
1 stick celery, chopped
1 red pepper, chopped
SWEET CURRY DRESSING
⅔ cup oil
⅓ cup white vinegar
1 tablespoon curry powder
¼ cup sugar

Add rice to large pan of boiling water, boil rapidly, uncovered, for about 30 minutes or until rice is tender. Drain rice, rinse under cold water; drain well.

Combine rice, tuna, apple, raisins, shallots, celery and pepper with Dressing in bowl; mix well.

Sweet Curry Dressing: Place all ingredients in jar; shake well.

Serves 4.

TUNA, PASTA AND BEAN SALAD WITH ANCHOVY DRESSING

2 x 425g cans tuna, drained
310g can cannellini beans, drained
½ cup chopped black olives
½ cup chopped green olives
250g pasta
1 tablespoon oil
1 bunch English spinach
ANCHOVY DRESSING
45g can anchovy fillets, drained, chopped
2 cloves garlic, crushed
1 small fresh red chilli, finely chopped
¼ cup lemon juice
¼ cup oil
1 teaspoon sugar

Combine tuna, rinsed beans and olives in bowl. Cook pasta in boiling water for about 10 minutes or until just tender; drain, place in bowl. Heat oil in pan, add spinach, cover, cook 2 minutes or until wilted, stir into pasta with tuna mixture; place on serving plates, top with Dressing.

Anchovy Dressing: Combine all ingredients; mix well.

Serves 6.

CRACKED WHEAT AND MINTED LAMB SALAD

Italian parsley is the flat-leafed variety.

3 racks lamb (4 cutlets in each)
1 cup cracked wheat (burghul)
½ cup brown sugar
¼ cup lemon juice
¼ cup oil
2 tablespoons mint jelly
2 cups chopped Italian parsley
2 cups chopped mint
1 apple, chopped
2 tomatoes, peeled, chopped
DRESSING
½ cup lemon juice
¼ cup oil
2 tablespoons mint jelly
2 cloves garlic, crushed

Cover wheat with boiling water, stand 15 minutes. Drain, rinse under cold water, spread out on absorbent paper.

Trim lamb, place in bowl, add combined sugar, lemon juice, oil and mint jelly, cover; marinate several hours, or refrigerate overnight.

Place lamb on rack over baking dish, bake in moderate oven 40 minutes, or until cooked as desired; baste several times with marinade during cooking. Stand meat 5 minutes before cutting into cutlets.

Combine wheat, parsley, mint, apple and tomatoes with Dressing, place onto plates; top with lamb.
Dressing: Combine all ingredients; serve immediately.

Serves 4 to 6.

BEEF 'N' AVOCADO SALAD WITH TARRAGON BEARNAISE SAUCE

The sauce can be made up to several hours beforehand if preferred; stand covered at room temperature.

1kg beef eye fillet (in one piece)
6 small beetroot
½ cup white vinegar
1 clove garlic, crushed
1 bay leaf
½ teaspoon ground allspice (or pimento)
60g butter
3 avocados, sliced
TARRAGON BEARNAISE SAUCE
¼ cup tarragon vinegar
5 egg yolks
250g butter, melted

Boil, steam or microwave unpeeled beetroot until tender; drain, peel, slice. Combine vinegar, garlic, bay leaf and allspice in pan, bring to boil, add beetroot; cool, stand overnight.

Tie beef securely with string to hold in shape while cooking. Melt butter in pan, add beef, cook over high heat, turning constantly until well browned; reduce heat, continue to cook until beef is cooked as desired. Cool beef, cut into thick slices. Place beef, beetroot and avocados on plates; top with Sauce just before serving.
Tarragon Bearnaise Sauce: Boil vinegar in small pan until reduced to about 2 tablespoons, cool. Blend or process egg yolks and vinegar until smooth, gradually pour in hot, bubbly butter while blender is operating.

Serves 6.

HAM AND CHEESE PARCELS WITH SOUR CREAM DRESSING

375g ham
200g gruyere cheese
4 sticks celery
4 green shallots
1 tablespoon oil
1 tablespoon lemon juice
2 lettuce
SOUR CREAM DRESSING
200g carton light sour cream
1 small onion, finely chopped
40g packet French onion soup
¼ cup French dressing
2 tablespoons chopped parsley

Cut ham, cheese, celery and shallots into thin 5cm lengths; place in bowl, add oil and lemon juice. Remove 12 large leaves from lettuce. Bring a large pan of water to the boil, add lettuce leaves, remove and drain. Immediately rinse under cold water; drain.

Divide ham mixture over lettuce leaves, roll up firmly. Serve topped with Dressing; serve immediately.
Sour Cream Dressing: Combine all ingredients; mix well.

Serves 4 to 6.

LEFT: Top: Red Salmon and Basil Salad; left: Tuna, Pasta and Bean Salad with Anchovy Dressing; right: Tuna and Rice Salad with Sweet Curry Dressing.
ABOVE: Top left: Cracked Wheat and Minted Lamb Salad; right: Beef 'n' Avocado Salad with Tarragon Bearnaise Sauce; bottom: Ham and Cheese Parcels with Sour Cream Dressing.

SHREDDED CHICKEN SALAD

6 chicken breast fillets
1 cup chicken stock
1 tablespoon oil
2 eggs, lightly beaten
2 pieces canned bamboo shoots
1 cup (100g) bean sprouts
DRESSING
½ cup French dressing
⅓ cup lemon juice
1 tablespoon sugar

Place stock in large pan. Add chicken, cover, bring to the boil, reduce heat, simmer 10 minutes or until chicken is tender; drain, cool. (Or, microwave chicken and stock, covered in shallow dish, on HIGH for about 5 minutes, or until chicken is tender.) Cut chicken into thin strips.

Heat oil in small pan, add eggs, cook without stirring until just set, turn omelet over, cook until firm; remove from pan, place on absorbent paper, cool. Cut omelet and bamboo shoots into thin strips, combine chicken, omelet, bamboo shoots, sprouts and Dressing in bowl; refrigerate several hours before serving.

Dressing: Combine all ingredients in jar; shake well.

Serves 4.

HOT HONEYED CHICKEN AND WALNUT SALAD

6 chicken breast fillets
3 carrots
3 sticks celery
3 onions
¾ cup (60g) walnut halves
¼ cup walnut oil
2 tablespoons chopped parsley
¼ cup honey
1½ tablespoons tomato sauce
½ teaspoon five spice powder

Cut chicken, carrots, celery and onions into thin strips. Toast walnuts on oven tray in moderate oven for 5 minutes.

Heat oil in pan, add chicken, cook until chicken is browned and just tender; remove from pan. Add carrots to pan, cook carrots until almost tender, add celery and onions, cook until onions are soft. Return chicken to pan, add parsley and combined honey, tomato sauce and five spice powder. Serve hot, sprinkled with walnuts.

Serves 4.

CHICKEN AND PINEAPPLE SALAD WITH CURRIED MAYONNAISE

1 barbecued chicken
½ cup shredded coconut
440g can unsweetened pineapple
    slices, drained
4 green shallots, chopped
CURRIED MAYONNAISE
1 teaspoon curry powder
¼ teaspoon five spice powder
1 clove garlic, crushed
1 teaspoon grated fresh ginger
¾ cup mayonnaise
¼ cup coconut milk

Toast coconut on oven tray in moderate oven for about 5 minutes. Cut chicken and pineapple into chunks; place in bowl, mix in coconut, shallots and Mayonnaise. Refrigerate 1 hour before serving.

Curried Mayonnaise: Combine all ingredients thoroughly.

Serves 4.

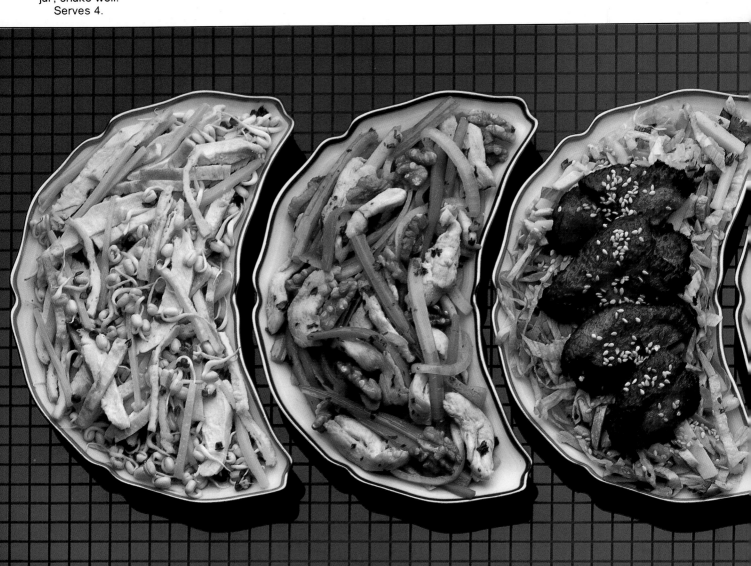

HOT CHICKEN AND CHILLI SALAD

We used the hot Asian variety of chilli sauce in this recipe.

No.15 chicken
2 tablespoons dry sherry
1 teaspoon sesame oil
1 tablespoon hoisin sauce
1 teaspoon chilli sauce
1 tablespoon oil
1 cup (125g) slivered almonds
½ cup sesame seeds
230g can sliced water chestnuts, drained
1 lettuce, shredded
2 tablespoons chopped fresh coriander
oil for deep frying
DRESSING
¼ cup lemon juice
2 tablespoons dry sherry
2 tablespoons oil
1 teaspoon grated fresh ginger
½ teaspoon sesame oil

Cut chicken into serving-sized pieces. Combine sherry, sesame oil, hoisin and chilli sauces with chicken; cover, marinate several hours.

Heat oil in pan, add almonds and sesame seeds, stir constantly over heat until golden brown; drain on absorbent paper.

Combine lettuce, almonds, sesame seeds, water chestnuts and coriander with Dressing, place onto serving plates. Deep fry chicken in hot oil, a few pieces at a time, until crisp and golden brown; serve hot over salad.
Dressing: Combine all ingredients.
Serves 4.

CHILLI CHICKEN SALAD

Make several hours ahead for maximum flavor. Sweet soy sauce is an Indonesian ingredient available in Asian stores; it is called Benteng Ketjap Asin. We have used two different types of oil in this recipe; the olive oil for flavor and a regular salad oil for lightness.

6 chicken breast fillets
2 teaspoons cornflour
1 tablespoon sweet soy sauce
1 tablespoon dry sherry
2 tablespoons sesame seeds
250g snow peas
1 tablespoon oil
230g can sliced water chestnuts, drained
6 green shallots, chopped
2 small fresh red chillies, chopped
DRESSING
⅓ cup olive oil
⅓ cup oil
2 tablespoons dry sherry
1 tablespoon lemon juice
1 tablespoon light soy sauce
1 teaspoon French mustard
1 teaspoon grated fresh ginger
1 teaspoon sambal oelek
1 teaspoon sugar
1 egg yolk

Cut chicken into thin strips. Combine cornflour, sweet soy sauce and sherry in bowl, add chicken, toss well. Toast sesame seeds by stirring in a heavy pan over heat, cool. Add topped and tailed snow peas to pan of boiling water, drain immediately, rinse under cold water until cold; drain.

Heat oil in pan or wok, add chicken in batches, stir-fry until light brown all over and tender, remove from pan; cool. Combine the chicken, sesame seeds, water chestnuts, shallots and chillies in bowl, stir in Dressing, refrigerate at least 1 hour before serving to allow flavor to develop. Add snow peas just before serving.
Dressing: Combine all ingredients in jar; shake well.
Serves 4.

LEFT: From left to right: Shredded Chicken Salad; Hot Honeyed Chicken and Walnut Salad; Hot Chicken and Chilli Salad; Chicken and Pineapple Salad with Curried Mayonnaise; Chilli Chicken Salad.

SMOKED TROUT AND RICE SALAD

Smoked trout can be bought whole, sliced or in fillets from delicatessens.

4 fillets (125g) smoked trout
2 tablespoons oil
60g butter
2 cloves garlic, crushed
1 onion, finely chopped
200g wild rice
1 litre (4 cups) chicken stock
1 cup dry white wine
1 cup long grain white rice
1 cup chicken stock, extra
425g can baby corn, drained
1 green pepper
4 green shallots
DRESSING
¼ cup lemon juice
¼ cup oil

Cut trout into thin strips. Heat oil and butter in pan, add garlic and onion, cook, stirring 2 minutes; add wild rice, stir until all the grains are coated with butter mixture. Add stock and wine, bring to the boil, reduce heat, cover, simmer 25 minutes. Add white rice and extra stock, simmer further 20 minutes, stirring occasionally until rice is tender and liquid absorbed. Cut corn, pepper and shallots diagonally, add trout and Dressing, mix well; stir into hot rice mixture. Serve hot or cold.
Dressing: Combine all ingredients in jar; shake well.

Serves 4.

MARINATED COLD FISH SALAD

We used bream fillets in this recipe and two oils in the Dressing, the olive is for flavor and the salad oil for lightness.

750g white fish fillets
¾ cup white vinegar
¼ cup sugar
2 tablespoons lemon juice
1 clove garlic, crushed
3 tomatoes, peeled, chopped
2 onions, thinly sliced
3 zucchini, thinly sliced
1 green pepper, thinly sliced
½ cup black olives, pitted
DRESSING
⅓ cup white vinegar
¼ cup oil
¼ cup olive oil
1 tablespoon sugar
1 tablespoon chopped fresh mint

Place fish in large pan, cover with water, bring to the boil, reduce heat, simmer, covered, for about 5 minutes, or until tender; drain. Remove bones from fish, cut fish into large chunks.

Combine fish, vinegar, sugar, lemon juice and garlic in bowl; cover, marinate 30 minutes, drain. Combine fish, tomatoes, onions, zucchini, pepper, olives and Dressing in bowl; refrigerate until serving time.
Dressing: Combine ingredients in jar; shake well.

Serves 6.

MINT AND GINGER LOBSTER SALAD

4 green lobster tails
¼ cup light soy sauce
¼ cup dry sherry
¼ cup lemon juice
¼ cup oil
2 tablespoons chopped mint
1 tablespoon grated fresh ginger
1 small fresh red chilli, finely chopped
4 red peppers
1 bunch watercress
2 tablespoons chopped mint, extra

Cut soft fins and shell away from underside of lobsters, gently ease flesh away from shell. Combine soy sauce, sherry, lemon juice, oil, mint, ginger and chilli in bowl; add lobster, cover, marinate several hours.

Cut peppers in half, grill, cut-side down for about 5 minutes, or until skin starts to blister; cool. Peel skin from peppers, slice peppers diagonally.

Remove lobster from marinade, place marinade in pan, bring to the boil, reduce heat; add lobster, simmer gently, turning often for about 5 minutes, or until lobster is just tender. Remove lobster from pan, cut into slices. Place watercress and peppers on serving plates, top with lobster. Add extra mint to remaining marinade, serve poured over lobster.

Serves 4.

SMOKED LAMB AND FENNEL WITH LEMON DRESSING

Sliced smoked lamb is available from some delicatessens.

500g sliced smoked lamb
1 cup (100g) pecan nuts
1 bunch radishes, sliced
2 cups watercress leaves
2 fennel bulbs, sliced
1 cos lettuce
LEMON DRESSING
¼ cup lemon juice
3 teaspoons seeded mustard
2 egg yolks
¾ cup oil

Tear lamb into bite-sized pieces. Toast pecan nuts on oven tray in moderate oven for about 5 minutes. Combine lamb, pecans, radishes, watercress and fennel; serve on lettuce, topped with Dressing.

Lemon Dressing: Blend or process lemon juice, mustard and egg yolks; with motor operating, slowly pour in oil in a thin stream.

Serves 4.

LEFT: Top: Marinated Cold Fish Salad; bottom left: Smoked Trout and Rice Salad; right: Mint and Ginger Lobster Salad. BELOW: From left to right: Smoked Lamb and Fennel with Lemon Dressing; Pork, Prunes and Apples with Warm Brandy Sauce; Meatball and Potato Salad with Tomato Puree.

PORK, PRUNES AND APPLES WITH WARM BRANDY SAUCE

6 small pork fillets
¾ cup pitted prunes, halved
1 apple, sliced
1 tablespoon oil
1 small lettuce, shredded
1 apple, peeled, grated, extra
1 tablespoon lemon juice
WARM BRANDY SAUCE
1 tablespoon oil
1 onion, finely chopped
2 tablespoons brandy
1 tablespoon redcurrant jelly
½ cup cream

Cut pork fillets halfway through lengthways, open out, pound each fillet until it is about 1cm thick. Place a row of prunes and sliced apple along the centre of each fillet, roll up, secure with toothpicks. Place in single layer in ovenproof dish, brush with oil, bake in moderate oven 30 minutes, or until pork is tender. Cool, then slice thinly.

Combine lettuce, grated apple and lemon juice in bowl, place on serving plates, top with pork and Sauce.

Warm Brandy Sauce: Heat oil in pan, add onion, cook, stirring, until onion is soft; stir in brandy and redcurrant jelly, bring to the boil, remove from heat; stir in cream, heat without boiling.

Serves 6.

MEATBALL AND POTATO SALAD WITH TOMATO PUREE

Taco seasoning mix can be bought in supermarkets or delicatessens.

375g minced beef
250g sausage mince
1 cup grated tasty cheese
35g sachet taco seasoning mix
1 egg
60g butter
500g baby new potatoes
425g can baby corn, drained
TOMATO PUREE
2 large ripe tomatoes, chopped
2 onions, chopped
1 red pepper, chopped
½ cup dry red wine

Combine minces, cheese, taco seasoning mix and egg; roll mixture into small balls. Melt butter in large pan, add meatballs, cook, stirring, over medium heat, until browned all over and cooked through. Remove from pan, drain, cool. Halve potatoes, boil or steam until tender; drain, cool. Combine meatballs, potatoes, and corn. Serve topped with Tomato Puree.

Tomato Puree: Combine all ingredients in pan, bring to the boil, reduce heat, simmer uncovered 20 minutes, or until mixture is thick. Blend or process mixture until smooth; strain, cool.

Serves 4.

SMOKED BEEF WITH TANGY YOGHURT DRESSING

Sliced smoked beef is available from some delicatessens.

375g sliced smoked beef
250g punnet cherry tomatoes, halved
6 hard-boiled eggs, quartered
1 cup alfalfa sprouts
4 spinach leaves, finely shredded
TANGY YOGHURT DRESSING
½ cup plain yoghurt
2 tablespoons cream
1 tablespoon chopped chives
1 teaspoon sugar

Arrange beef, tomatoes, eggs and sprouts over spinach on serving plates; top with Dressing.

Tangy Yoghurt Dressing: Blend or process all ingredients until smooth.
Serves 6.

LEFT: Smoked Beef with Tangy Yoghurt Dressing.
BELOW: Clockwise from top: Hot Prawn and Bacon Salad with Mustard Dressing; Squid and Zucchini Salad with Avocado Dressing; Seafood and Baby New Potato Salad; Mussel and Bacon Salad with Devilled Dressing.

MUSSEL AND BACON SALAD WITH DEVILLED DRESSING

Cooked mussel meat or frozen "Kiwi Clams" are available from large seafood shops. If unavailable, substitute two and a half kg mussels in the shell. To cook mussels, place them into pan of boiling water, boil until the shells open. Remove mussels from opened shells, discard any unopened mussels.

750g cooked mussel meat
500g broccoli
5 slices wholemeal bread
2 tablespoons pine nuts
3 bacon rashers, chopped
DEVILLED DRESSING
⅓ cup oil
2 tablespoons lemon juice
2 tablespoons tomato sauce
1 tablespoon sour cream
2 teaspoons Worcestershire sauce
1 teaspoon French mustard
few drops tabasco sauce
½ teaspoon sugar
1 egg yolk

Cut broccoli into flowerets, boil, steam or microwave until just tender; drain, rinse under cold water; drain. Remove crusts from bread, cut bread into cubes. Toast cubes on oven tray in moderate oven for about 5 minutes, add pine nuts to tray, bake further 5 minutes, or until bread and pine nuts are golden brown; cool. Cook bacon in pan until crisp; drain on absorbent paper. Combine mussels, broccoli, pine nuts and bacon with Dressing in bowl. Place onto plates, sprinkle with cubes of toast just before serving.

Devilled Dressing: Whisk all ingredients together in bowl.
Serves 4.

22

HOT PRAWN AND BACON SALAD WITH MUSTARD DRESSING

500g cooked king prawns
4 bacon rashers
500g baby new potatoes
15g butter
1 small red pepper, chopped
1 small green pepper, chopped
250g baby mushrooms, halved
2 tablespoons chopped chives
MUSTARD DRESSING
2 teaspoons seeded mustard
⅓ cup oil
2 tablespoons white vinegar
1 clove garlic, crushed

Shell and devein prawns, cut each bacon rasher into three pieces. Wrap each prawn in a piece of bacon, secure with toothpicks. Boil, steam or microwave potatoes until tender; drain, cut in half. Melt butter in pan, add prawns, cook until bacon is browned; remove rolls from pan, remove toothpicks. Add potatoes and peppers to pan, stir-fry for a few minutes, add prawns, mushrooms, chives and Dressing, stir-fry until heated through.

Mustard Dressing: Combine all ingredients in jar; shake well.

Serves 4.

SEAFOOD AND BABY NEW POTATO SALAD

500g (about 6) small squid
500g cooked king prawns
500g baby new potatoes
¼ cup French dressing
1 teaspoon French mustard
2 tablespoons chopped parsley
2 tablespoons mayonnaise
1 teaspoon French mustard, extra
1 tablespoon chopped fresh dill

Clean squid, cut into rings. Add squid to pan of boiling water, return water to the boil, drain immediately. Shell and devein prawns.

Boil, steam or microwave potatoes until tender; drain, cool slightly, cut into thick slices. Combine potatoes in bowl with dressing, mustard and parsley. Combine mayonnaise, extra mustard and dill with squid and prawns. Place potato and seafood mixture onto plates, serve warm or cold.

Serves 4.

SQUID AND ZUCCHINI SALAD WITH AVOCADO DRESSING

750g small squid tubes
6 small zucchini
2 red peppers
60g butter
¼ cup chopped chives
2 cups (200g) bean sprouts
AVOCADO DRESSING
1 ripe avocado
¼ cup French dressing
¼ cup water
1 clove garlic, crushed

Trim ends from squid tubes, cut tubes in half lengthways. Using a sharp knife score inside of tubes in a diamond pattern; do not cut through. Drop squid into pan of boiling water, return to boil; drain immediately, rinse under cold water. Cut zucchini and peppers into long thin strips. Melt butter in pan, add zucchini, peppers and chives, saute until peppers are just tender, add bean sprouts, remove from heat. Place onto serving plates, top with squid, then Dressing; serve immediately.

Avocado Dressing: Blend or process all ingredients until smooth.

Serves 6.

ITALIAN BEAN AND MUSHROOM SALAD WITH BASIL DRESSING

Make up to three days in advance if preferred; keep refrigerated.

125g thinly sliced salami
2 x 432g cans red kidney beans, drained
2 x 310g butter beans, drained
250g baby mushrooms, sliced
12 pitted black olives, sliced
4 green shallots, chopped
250g punnet cherry tomatoes, halved
BASIL DRESSING
½ cup olive oil
¼ cup red wine vinegar
1 clove garlic, crushed
1 tablespoon chopped fresh basil

Cut salami into strips. Combine rinsed beans in bowl with salami, mushrooms, olives, shallots and Dressing; cover, refrigerate overnight. Add tomatoes just before serving.

Basil Dressing: Combine all ingredients in jar; shake well.

Serves 4.

MARINATED SESAME LAMB AND VEGETABLE SALAD

750g lamb fillets
1 tablespoon oil
500g baby new potatoes
½ small cauliflower
2 sticks celery, sliced
425g can baby corn, sliced
2 tablespoons toasted sesame sèeds
MARINADE
¼ cup light soy sauce
1 clove garlic, crushed
2 teaspoons sugar
½ teaspoon sesame oil
DRESSING
2 tablespoons light soy sauce
1 tablespoon dry sherry
1 teaspoon sugar
¼ teaspoon sesame oil

Remove fat and sinew from lamb, cut across the grain into thin diagonal slices. Combine lamb with Marinade, stand several hours or, refrigerate overnight; drain; discard Marinade.

Heat oil in large pan, add half the lamb, stir over high heat until lamb is well browned all over, remove from pan. Repeat with remaining lamb.

Boil, steam or microwave potatoes until tender; drain, rinse under cold water; drain. Cut cauliflower into flowerets, boil, steam or microwave until just tender; drain, rinse under cold water; drain. Combine potatoes, cauliflower, celery and corn with lamb, add Dressing. Place onto serving plates; sprinkle with sesame seeds just before serving.

Marinade: Combine all ingredients.
Dressing: Combine all ingredients in jar; shake well.

Serves 6.

CURRIED PORK SALAD WITH APPLE CIDER DRESSING

750g pork fillets
1 tablespoon curry powder
2 tablespoons oil
1 apple, thinly sliced
2 sticks celery, chopped
3 cucumbers, sliced
6 green shallots, chopped
2 tablespoons chopped parsley
1 tablespoon sultanas
APPLE CIDER DRESSING
2 tablespoons cider vinegar
⅓ cup apple juice
200g carton sour cream
1 clove garlic, crushed

Rub pork fillets with curry powder. Heat oil in pan, add pork, cook over high heat, turning often, until browned all over; reduce heat, cook until tender, remove from pan, cool.

Combine apple, celery, cucumbers, shallots, parsley and sultanas in bowl, add Dressing, toss well. Slice pork, mix into salad, refrigerate about 2 hours before serving.

Apple Cider Dressing: Combine all ingredients; mix well.

Serves 6.

WARM ROAST DUCK SALAD WITH PEACH SAUCE

No. 15 duck
840g can sliced peaches, drained
60g butter
1 large onion, chopped
6 large spinach leaves, chopped
½ teaspoon nutmeg
½ small red pepper, chopped
PEACH SAUCE
2 cloves garlic, crushed
2 teaspoons grated fresh ginger
¼ cup lemon juice
2 tablespoons honey
2 teaspoons light soy sauce

Place duck on rack over baking dish, bake in moderate oven 1 hour, or until duck is tender. Wrap duck in foil, keep warm. Drain peaches, reserve ½ cup syrup for Sauce.

Melt butter in pan, add onion, cook until onion is soft, add spinach, nutmeg and pepper; stir over heat until spinach is just wilted. Serve sliced duck, with remaining peaches over spinach, top with warm Sauce.

Peach Sauce: Combine garlic, ginger, lemon juice, honey, soy sauce, the reserved syrup and the remaining half of the peach slices in blender or processor, puree until smooth; heat in pan.

Serves 4.

RIGHT: Clockwise from top right: Marinated Sesame Lamb and Vegetable Salad; Curried Pork Salad with Apple Cider Dressing; Warm Roast Duck Salad with Peach Sauce; Italian Bean and Mushroom Salad with Basil Dressing.

TOP DRESSINGS

These recipes are some of our favorites, from the classics through to a deliciously light dressing for slimmers.

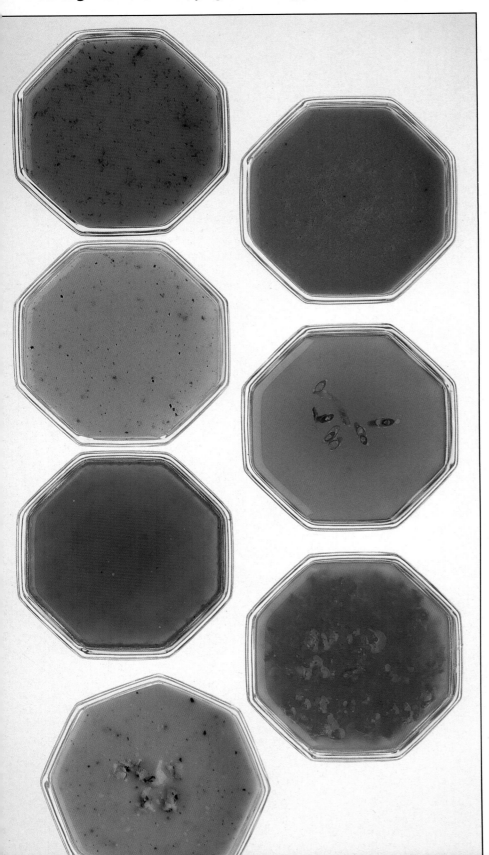

HERBED DRESSING
¾ cup oil
¼ cup white vinegar
1 tablespoon chopped fresh basil
1 tablespoon chopped parsley
½ teaspoon dried oregano leaves
Combine ingredients in jar; shake well.
Makes 1 cup.

LO- JOULE TOMATO DRESSING
1 large (150g) tomato, peeled
½ cup lo-joule coleslaw dressing
1 tablespoon tomato paste
2 teaspoons Worcestershire sauce
2 tablespoons lemon juice
1 clove garlic, crushed
Remove seeds from tomato, roughly chop tomato. Blend or process all ingredients until smooth. Approximately 40kJ per tablespoon.
Makes 1 cup.

CURRIED FRENCH DRESSING
¾ cup oil
¼ cup white vinegar
2 teaspoons curry powder
2 green shallots, chopped
Combine ingredients in jar; shake well.
Makes 1 cup.

ITALIAN DRESSING
⅔ cup olive oil
⅓ cup white vinegar
2 cloves garlic, crushed
1 small onion, finely chopped
1 tablespoon finely chopped canned or bottled red pimiento
Combine ingredients in jar; shake well.
Makes 1 cup.

ROQUEFORT DRESSING
¼ cup white vinegar
¼ cup lemon juice
½ cup oil
75g roquefort cheese
2 tablespoons cream
Combine vinegar and lemon juice in bowl, gradually whisk in oil. Whisk in crumbled cheese and cream.
Makes 1 cup.

HOT SWEET DRESSING
½ cup oil
¼ cup white vinegar
¼ cup sweet chilli sauce
1 teaspoon sugar
Combine ingredients in jar; shake well.
Makes 1 cup.

FRENCH DRESSING
⅔ cup oil
⅓ cup white vinegar or lemon juice
¼ teaspoon dry mustard
Combine ingredients in jar; shake well.
Makes 1 cup.

Dressings clockwise from top left: Herbed; Lo-Joule Tomato; Curried French; Italian; Roquefort; Hot Sweet; French.

GOOD COMPANIONS

Top-notch team mates for hot or cold chicken, meat or fish, these dishes illustrate the versatility of accompanying salads. Serve a selection at a barbecue or buffet meal; let everyone mix and match.

BELOW: Back: Hot Creamy Tomato Pasta and Pepperoni Salad; front: Curried Pasta Salad.

CURRIED PASTA SALAD
375g pasta shells
1 teaspoon oil
250g baby mushrooms, halved
1 green pepper, chopped
3 green shallots, chopped
2 sticks celery, sliced
DRESSING
½ cup oil
½ cup white vinegar
2 tablespoons sugar
1½ tablespoons curry powder

Add pasta gradually to large pan of boiling water, boil rapidly, uncovered, for about 10 minutes or until just tender; drain, rinse under cold water. Mix oil through pasta with hands.

Combine pasta in bowl with remaining ingredients and Dressing. Refrigerate 1 hour or overnight.

Dressing: Combine all ingredients in jar; shake well.

Serves 6.

HOT CREAMY TOMATO PASTA AND PEPPERONI SALAD
250g spiral pasta
15g butter
1 onion, thinly sliced
100g pepperoni salami, thinly sliced
400g can tomatoes, drained
½ cup cream
½ teaspoon ground oregano
1 tablespoon chopped parsley

Add pasta gradually to a large pan of boiling water, boil rapidly, uncovered, for about 10 minutes or until just tender; drain. Heat butter in large pan, add onion and pepperoni, cook, stirring, a few minutes or until onion is lightly browned. Add the crushed tomatoes, bring to the boil, reduce heat, simmer uncovered for a few minutes. Remove from heat, stir in cream, oregano and parsley, then pasta; mix well. Heat gently; serve immediately.

Serves 6.

TWO-CABBAGE SALAD WITH LEMON MUSTARD DRESSING

¼ red cabbage, shredded
¼ white cabbage, shredded
6 slices white bread
1 tablespoon oil
30g butter
1 teaspoon paprika
4 bacon rashers, chopped
LEMON MUSTARD DRESSING
2 tablespoons lemon juice
2 tablespoons lemon flavored
    mustard
1 tablespoon dry white wine
¼ cup oil

Mix cabbages together in bowl. Remove crusts from bread, cut bread into small cubes. Heat oil and butter in pan, add paprika and bread, cook, stirring, until bread is crisp; drain on absorbent paper. Fry bacon in pan until crisp; drain. Add the bread, bacon and hot Dressing to cabbage mixture, then mix lightly; serve immediately.

Lemon Mustard Dressing: Combine lemon juice, mustard and wine in pan, place over medium heat. Whisk in oil gradually, whisk until smooth and slightly thickened; do not boil.

Serves 6.

BELOW: Two-Cabbage Salad with Lemon Mustard Dressing.
RIGHT: From top: Hot Glazed Sweet Red Coleslaw; Corn and Pimiento Salad with Tarragon Dressing; Cucumber Salad with Avocado Dill Dressing; Baby Squash Salad with Creamy Chive Dressing; Minted Tomato and Pea Salad.

CUCUMBER SALAD WITH AVOCADO DILL DRESSING

Prepare Dressing just before serving, or avocado will discolor.

3 cucumbers, peeled, sliced
⅔ cup white vinegar
½ cup sugar
2 cups watercress leaves, chopped
AVOCADO DILL DRESSING
1 avocado
¼ cup cream
¼ cup mayonnaise
1 tablespoon lemon juice
1 tablespoon chopped fresh dill

Combine cucumber, vinegar and sugar in bowl, stand 20 minutes; drain. Combine cucumber, watercress and Dressing in bowl; serve immediately.

Avocado Dill Dressing: Blend or process avocado with cream, mayonnaise, lemon juice and dill until smooth.

Serves 6.

HOT GLAZED SWEET RED COLESLAW

1 tablespoon oil
30g butter
1 small onion, chopped
½ red cabbage, shredded
½ cup port
½ cup fruit chutney
¼ cup dry white wine
¼ cup brown sugar

Heat oil and butter in large pan, add onion, cook, stirring, until onion is just soft; add cabbage, cook, stirring, few minutes, or until cabbage is just wilted. Stir in combined port, chutney, wine and sugar, bring to the boil, reduce heat, simmer 20 minutes, uncovered, or until liquid is reduced and cabbage glazed; serve immediately.

Serves 6.

BABY SQUASH SALAD WITH CREAMY CHIVE DRESSING

500g baby green squash, quartered
500g baby yellow squash, quartered
125g ham, chopped
2 apples, sliced
CREAMY CHIVE DRESSING
⅓ cup cream
¼ cup mayonnaise
1 tablespoon chopped chives

Boil, steam or microwave squash until just tender; drain, rinse under cold water; drain. Combine squash, ham, apples and Dressing in bowl, mix well; serve immediately.

Creamy Chive Dressing: Combine all ingredients thoroughly.

Serves 6.

MINTED TOMATO AND PEA SALAD

500g (3 cups) fresh or frozen peas
1 cucumber
4 green shallots, chopped
250g punnet cherry tomatoes
DRESSING
½ cup oil
¼ cup white vinegar
1 tablespoon chopped mint
1 clove garlic, crushed

Boil, steam or microwave peas until tender; drain, rinse under cold water; drain. Cut cucumber in half lengthways, remove seeds, slice cucumber thinly. Combine peas, cucumber, shallots and quartered tomatoes in bowl with Dressing; serve immediately.

Dressing: Combine all ingredients in jar; shake well.

Serves 4.

CORN AND PIMIENTO SALAD WITH TARRAGON DRESSING

May be made the day before required. Canned or bottled red peppers (or pimientos) are an imported product available from delicatessens.

2 x 440g cans corn kernels, drained
340g jar pimientos (red peppers)
    drained, chopped
2 tablespoons chopped parsley
1 green pepper, chopped
4 green shallots, chopped
TARRAGON DRESSING
⅓ cup olive oil
2 tablespoons tarragon vinegar
1 teaspoon French mustard
½ teaspoon dried tarragon leaves

Combine corn, pimientos, parsley, pepper, shallots and Dressing in bowl, toss well; refrigerate 1 hour or overnight before serving.

Tarragon Dressing: Combine all ingredients in jar; shake well.

Serves 6.

ORIENTAL VEGETABLE SALAD

⅓ cup slivered almonds
2 tablespoons sesame seeds
5 cups (500g) bean sprouts
500g cooked prawns, shelled
250g baby mushrooms, sliced
6 green shallots, finely sliced
DRESSING
½ cup oil
½ teaspoon sesame oil
1 tablespoon white vinegar
2 tablespoons lemon juice
2 teaspoons light soy sauce
1 teaspoon sugar

Toast almonds on oven tray in moderate oven for about 5 minutes; cool. Toast sesame seeds by stirring over heat in heavy pan, remove from pan; cool. Combine the almonds, sesame seeds, bean sprouts, chopped prawns, mushrooms and shallots in bowl. Add Dressing, toss well; refrigerate 1 hour before serving.

Dressing: Combine all ingredients in jar; shake well.

Serves 6.

GREEN BEAN SALAD WITH GINGER DRESSING

If using fresh young stringless beans it is unnecessary to cook them before using. Rice vinegar is available from Asian stores; use cider vinegar as a substitute if preferred.

1 tablespoon sesame seeds
1 kg green beans
1 onion, sliced
GINGER DRESSING
⅓ cup oil
¼ teaspoon sesame oil
2 tablespoons rice vinegar
1 teaspoon grated fresh ginger

Toast sesame seeds by stirring over heat in heavy pan, remove from pan; cool. Top and tail beans. Boil, steam or microwave beans until bright green, and just tender; drain, place into bowl of iced water, stand until beans are completely cold; drain. Combine sesame seeds, beans, onion and Dressing in bowl; refrigerate 1 hour or overnight before serving.

Ginger Dressing: Combine all ingredients in jar; shake well.

Serves 6.

FRIED BROWN RICE SALAD

2 cups brown rice
4 bacon rashers, chopped
250g baby mushrooms, sliced
1 large carrot, coarsely grated
125g snow peas, chopped
4 green shallots, chopped
DRESSING
½ cup oil
¼ cup brown vinegar
2 teaspoons light soy sauce
½ teaspoon sesame oil

Add rice gradually to large pan of boiling water, boil rapidly, uncovered, for about 30 minutes or until tender; drain, rinse under cold water; drain.

Fry bacon in large pan until crisp, add mushrooms, carrot and snow peas, stir-fry until snow peas are just tender. Add shallots, rice and Dressing, stir-fry until rice is heated through; serve hot or cold.

Dressing: Combine all ingredients in jar; shake well.

Serves 6.

BROWN RICE AND CUCUMBER SALAD WITH TZATZIKI DRESSING

Salad may be made the day before required. You will need to boil 1½ cups rice for this recipe.

5 cups cooked brown rice
4 cucumbers, chopped
1 red pepper, chopped
2 sticks celery, sliced
6 green shallots, chopped
2 tablespoons coarsely grated
  parmesan cheese
TZATZIKI DRESSING
⅓ cup olive oil
2 tablespoons cider vinegar
2 tablespoons plain yoghurt
1 teaspoon French mustard
2 cloves garlic, crushed
1 teaspoon sugar
Combine rice, cucumbers, pepper, celery, shallots and cheese in bowl, add Dressing; toss well. Refrigerate 1 hour or overnight before serving.
Tzatziki Dressing: Combine all ingredients thoroughly.

Serves 6.

LEFT: Top left: Green Bean Salad with Ginger Dressing; right: Oriental Vegetable Salad; bottom: Fried Brown Rice Salad.

TOASTED BUCKWHEAT AND CHICK PEA SALAD WITH MINT DRESSING

Canned chick peas are an imported product available at delicatessens. If using dried chick peas, you will need to soak one cup chick peas in cold water overnight. Next day, boil the peas in fresh water for about one hour, or until tender; drain, cool. We have used two types of oil in this recipe; the olive oil for flavor and a salad oil for lightness.

1 tablespoon oil
2 cloves garlic, crushed
½ cup cracked buckwheat
410g can chick peas, drained
2 tomatoes, peeled, chopped
2 green peppers, chopped
MINT DRESSING
2 tablespoons lemon juice
1 tablespoon dry white wine
1 tablespoon olive oil
1 tablespoon oil
1 tablespoon chopped mint
Heat oil in pan, add garlic and buckwheat, cook, stirring, a few minutes or until buckwheat is golden brown; cool.

Combine buckwheat, rinsed chick peas, tomatoes, peppers and Dressing in bowl; refrigerate several hours or overnight before serving.
Mint Dressing: Combine all ingredients thoroughly.

Serves 6.

PEPPER AND AVOCADO SALAD WITH PARMESAN DRESSING

2 tablespoons sesame seeds
2 red peppers
4 spinach leaves, shredded
1 small lettuce, shredded
6 green shallots, chopped
2 avocados, sliced
PARMESAN DRESSING
½ cup oil
¼ cup white vinegar
⅓ cup grated fresh parmesan cheese
Toast sesame seeds by stirring over heat in heavy pan, remove from pan immediately; cool.

Cut peppers in half, place under hot griller, skin side up, until skin blisters. Remove and discard skins. Cut grilled peppers into thin strips.

Combine spinach, lettuce and shallots with Dressing in bowl. Top with avocado and peppers, sprinkle with sesame seeds; serve immediately.
Parmesan Dressing: Combine all ingredients in jar; shake well.

Serves 6.

ABOVE: Top left: Brown Rice and Cucumber Salad with Tzatziki Dressing; right: Toasted Buckwheat and Chick Pea Salad with Mint Dressing; bottom: Pepper and Avocado Salad with Parmesan Dressing.

BEETROOT AND FENNEL SALAD WITH ANCHOVY DRESSING

2 beetroot
2 fennel bulbs
1 red onion, sliced
radicchio lettuce
ANCHOVY DRESSING
½ cup lemon juice
45g can anchovy fillets, drained
2 tablespoons chopped fresh basil
2 tablespoons oil
½ teaspoon sugar

Peel beetroot, cut into thin strips 5cm long. Place beetroot in pan, cover with cold water, bring to the boil, reduce heat, simmer 3 minutes; drain, rinse under cold water; drain. Cut fennel into thin strips 5cm long. Place in pan, cover with cold water, bring to the boil, reduce heat, simmer 2 minutes; drain, rinse under cold water; drain.

Combine beetroot, fennel and onion in bowl with Dressing. Place radicchio in bowl, top with beetroot mixture; serve immediately.

Anchovy Dressing: Blend or process all ingredients until smooth.

Serves 6.

BELOW: Top left: Hot Potato and Ham Salad with Cream Cheese Dressing; right: Hot Layered Potato and Cabbage Salad; bottom: Beetroot and Fennel Salad with Anchovy Dressing.

HOT LAYERED POTATO AND CABBAGE SALAD

Red or white cabbage can be used.

½ cabbage, shredded
750g new potatoes, thickly sliced
300g carton sour cream
1 tablespoon brown vinegar
1 teaspoon sugar
1 tablespoon oil
1 onion, finely chopped
125g ham, chopped
1 cup grated tasty cheese

Boil, steam or microwave cabbage until just tender; drain. Boil, steam or microwave potatoes until tender; drain. Combine sour cream, vinegar and sugar in bowl. Heat oil in pan, add onion and ham, cook, stirring constantly, for a few minutes or until onion is golden brown.

Place half the cabbage in an ovenproof dish, top with half the potato, then half the sour cream mixture; repeat layers. Top with onion mixture and cheese. Bake in moderately hot oven for 15 minutes, or until golden brown; serve immediately.

Serves 6.

HOT POTATO AND HAM SALAD WITH CREAM CHEESE DRESSING

We used a hot Asian chilli sauce.

500g baby new potatoes
2 teaspoons oil
1 red onion, sliced
3 hard-boiled eggs, quartered
125g ham, chopped
CREAM CHEESE DRESSING
125g packet cream cheese
200g carton sour cream
1 teaspoon chilli sauce
2 tablespoons chopped mint

Boil, steam or microwave potatoes until tender; drain, cut into halves or quarters. Heat oil in pan, add onion, cook, stirring, until lightly browned. Combine hot potatoes, eggs and ham in bowl, add Dressing, sprinkle with onions; serve immediately.

Cream Cheese Dressing: Process chopped cream cheese, chilli sauce, sour cream and mint until smooth.

Serves 6.

RIGHT: From top: Hot Carrot and Parsnip Salad with Honey Dressing; Hot Stir-Fried Vegetable Salad with Orange Dressing; Orange and Onion Salad.

HOT CARROT AND PARSNIP SALAD WITH HONEY DRESSING
4 carrots
4 parsnips
60g butter
½ cup slivered almonds
HONEY DRESSING
2 tablespoons lemon juice
2 tablespoons honey
2 tablespoons seeded mustard
Coarsely grate carrots and parsnips. Heat butter in large pan, add almonds, cook, stirring constantly, until almonds are golden; drain on absorbent paper.

Add carrots and parsnips to pan, cook, stirring constantly, for about 5 minutes or until vegetables are just tender. Stir in Dressing; serve immediately sprinkled with almonds.

Honey Dressing: Combine all ingredients thoroughly.

Serves 6.

HOT STIR-FRIED VEGETABLE SALAD WITH ORANGE DRESSING
2 sticks celery
250g green beans
125g snow peas
¼ cup olive oil
1 onion, coarsely sliced
1 red pepper, sliced
ORANGE DRESSING
2 teaspoons grated orange rind
¼ cup orange juice
2 tablespoons chopped parsley
1 clove garlic, crushed
2 small fresh red chillies, chopped
Cut celery and beans into 5cm lengths. Top and tail snow peas. Heat oil in pan, add celery, beans and onion, cook, stirring, until vegetables are almost tender. Add pepper, snow peas and Dressing, stir-fry until hot; serve immediately.

Orange Dressing: Combine all ingredients in jar; shake well.

Serves 4.

ORANGE AND ONION SALAD
6 oranges
1 onion, sliced
1 cup watercress leaves
1 cup roasted unsalted cashews
DRESSING
2 teaspoons grated orange rind
¼ cup orange juice
1 egg yolk
1 tablespoon white vinegar
⅓ cup oil
Peel oranges thickly, removing all white pith. Segment by cutting down next to adjoining membrane to release the segments.

Combine orange segments, onion, watercress and cashews in bowl with Dressing; serve immediately.

Dressing: Blend or process orange rind and juice, egg yolk and vinegar until combined. With motor operating, gradually add oil constantly in a thin stream until mixture thickens.

Serves 4.

SEAFOOD ENTREES

The wonderful variety of fresh and easily obtained Australian seafood gives great scope to the imaginative cook. Seafood makes a light, elegant and nutritious entree and can be presented in many ways such as pates, soups and curries; it can be served cold, warm or hot.

CLAM BISQUE

Make your own fish stock by boiling several small fish heads (or pieces) in water for an hour. Cool stock; strain. Or crumble one or two chicken stock cubes in four cups hot water.

3 x 290g cans clams, drained
60g butter
2 onions, chopped
4 green shallots, chopped
4 bacon rashers, chopped
4 cups fish or chicken stock
1 cup dry white wine
300g carton sour cream
1 teaspoon turmeric
3 bacon rashers, extra
½ cup sour cream, extra

Rinse clams under cold water; drain. Reserve about one third of the clams. Heat butter in pan, add onions and shallots, cook 2 minutes, stirring. Add bacon, cook, stirring, 3 minutes. Add clams, stock and wine, bring to the boil, reduce heat, simmer uncovered 15 minutes. Remove from heat, add sour cream and turmeric. Blend or process mixture in several batches until smooth. Return mixture to pan, reheat without boiling. Cut extra bacon into 5cm lengths, add a few reserved clams to each bacon piece, roll up, secure with toothpicks; grill bacon rolls until crisp. Serve soup topped with extra sour cream and bacon rolls.
Serves 6.

CREAMY MUSSEL SOUP WITH FRIED GARLIC BREAD

18 mussels
15g butter
1 onion, finely chopped
2 bacon rashers, finely chopped
1 clove garlic, crushed
½ cup dry white wine
2 tablespoons lemon juice
1½ cups water
2 tablespoons fresh basil leaves
300ml carton cream
2 egg yolks
FRIED GARLIC BREAD
1 small French loaf, sliced
60g butter
1 clove garlic, crushed

Scrub and remove beards from mussels. Heat butter in pan, add onion, bacon and garlic, cook, stirring, 5 minutes; drain on absorbent paper. Combine wine, lemon juice and water in large pan, bring to the boil. Add mussels to pan, cover, cook few minutes or until mussels open. Remove mussels from pan, discard any that remain closed. Simmer remaining liquid few minutes, then pour into clean pan, leaving any grit and sand behind. Remove one shell from each mussel leaving mussel attached to the other remaining shell.

Cut basil leaves into strips, add onion mixture to liquid in pan with cream and basil, bring to the boil, reduce heat, simmer uncovered 10 minutes. Remove from heat, whisk in egg yolks. Place mussels into serving plates, top with hot soup, serve with Bread.
Fried Garlic Bread: Heat butter in pan, add garlic and bread slices in single layer, fry bread on both sides until golden brown.
Serves 4.

RIGHT: Back: Creamy Mussel Soup with Fried Garlic Bread; front: Clam Bisque.

SARDINE AND LIME PATE

Make one day in advance if preferred.

½ cup parsley sprigs
60g butter
60g packaged cream cheese
1 tablespoon lime juice
few drops tabasco sauce
110g can sardines, drained

Blend or process parsley until coarsely chopped, add butter, cream cheese, lime juice and tabasco; process until smooth. Place sardines on absorbent paper to absorb as much oil as possible. Mash sardines in bowl with a fork, stir in parsley mixture. Serve with toast or savory biscuits.

Serves 4.

SALMON LOAF WITH FRESH HERB MAYONNAISE

440g can red salmon, drained
2 cups stale breadcrumbs
2 sticks celery, finely chopped
4 green shallots, finely chopped
3 eggs, separated
1 teaspoon dry mustard
2 tablespoons lemon juice
1 teaspoon Worcestershire sauce
½ cup milk
15g butter
FRESH HERB MAYONNAISE
1 tablespoon chopped parsley
1 tablespoon chopped mint
1 tablespoon chopped chives
1 tablespoon chopped dill
½ cup mayonnaise
¼ cup French dressing
¼ cup cream
2 tablespoons lemon juice
1 teaspoon seeded mustard

Combine salmon, breadcrumbs, egg yolks, celery, shallots, mustard, lemon juice and Worcestershire sauce in bowl; mix well. Place milk in pan, bring to the boil, remove from heat, add butter; cool to warm. Stir milk mixture into salmon mixture. Beat egg whites in small bowl with electric mixer until firm peaks form; fold through salmon mixture. Pour mixture into greased loaf-shaped ovenproof dish (base measures 11cm x 18cm). Bake in moderate oven 50 minutes or until firm to touch. Cool in tin 10 minutes before turning onto serving plate. Serve warm with Mayonnaise.

Fresh Herb Mayonnaise: Combine all ingredients thoroughly.

Serves 6.

ABOVE: Top: Smoked Trout and Bearnaise Sauce Pate; bottom left: Sardine and Lime Pate; right: Salmon Loaf with Fresh Herb Mayonnaise.
RIGHT: Lobster Salad with Saffron Mayonnaise.

SMOKED TROUT AND BEARNAISE SAUCE PATE

If whole smoked trout are unavailable, 500g of packaged smoked trout or cooked smoked cod can be used as a substitute if preferred.

2 large whole smoked trout
2 teaspoons gelatine
2 tablespoons water
4 green shallots, chopped
BEARNAISE SAUCE
¼ cup tarragon vinegar
3 egg yolks
125g butter, melted

Remove skin from trout, carefully pull flesh away from bones, remove all bones, flake flesh with fork. Sprinkle gelatine over water, dissolve over hot water (or microwave on HIGH 30 seconds); cool to room temperature.

Combine trout, gelatine mixture, shallots and Sauce in bowl, pour into individual dishes, refrigerate several hours or overnight. Remove from refrigerator 1 hour before serving.

Bearnaise Sauce: Heat vinegar in small pan, boil until reduced to about 2 tablespoons. Blend or process egg yolks and vinegar until smooth, gradually pour in hot, bubbling butter while motor is operating.

Serves 6.

LOBSTER SALAD WITH SAFFRON MAYONNAISE

Mayonnaise can be made up to a week ahead if preferred.

2 small lobsters
SAFFRON MAYONNAISE
¼ cup brandy
1 clove garlic, crushed
3 egg yolks
1 teaspoon French mustard
2 teaspoons tarragon vinegar
½ cup oil
tiny pinch saffron powder
¼ cup sour cream
1 tablespoon chopped capers
1 tablespoon chopped chives

Cut lobsters in half, remove lobster meat, wash shells. Slice lobster, return to shells, top with Mayonnaise, refrigerate several hours before serving.

Saffron Mayonnaise: Combine brandy and garlic in pan, bring to the boil, reduce heat, simmer until liquid is reduced to about 1 tablespoon; strain through fine sieve. Blend or process brandy mixture with egg yolks, mustard and vinegar until smooth. Add oil gradually in a thin stream while motor is operating; add saffron, sour cream, capers and chives, blend 30 seconds.

Serves 4.

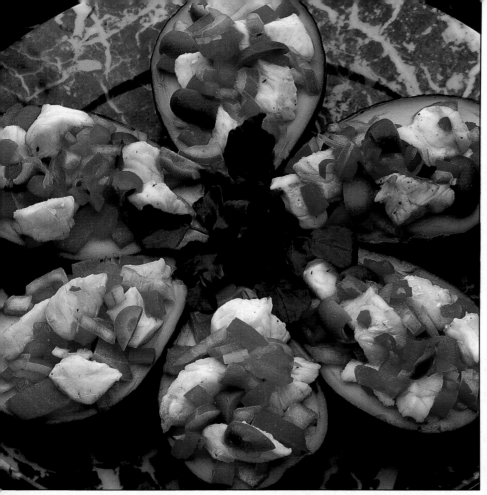

place right way up on oven tray. Add Filling to "baskets"; sprinkle with Topping. Bake in moderately hot oven 5 minutes or until Topping is golden brown; serve immediately.

Filling: Place water in pan, bring to the boil, add scallops, return to the boil, drain; reserve 1 cup of the liquid. Melt butter in pan, add garlic, flour and mustard, stir over heat 1 minute. Gradually add reserved liquid, stir constantly over heat until mixture boils and thickens. Stir in cream, egg yolks, lemon juice and scallops.

Topping: Melt butter, stir in breadcrumbs, chives and lemon rind.

Serves 6.

LEMON SAFFRON CREPES WITH SEAFOOD FILLING

LEMON SAFFRON CREPES
¾ cup plain flour
3 eggs, lightly beaten
2 teaspoons grated lemon rind
½ cup lemon juice
½ cup milk
tiny pinch saffron powder
SEAFOOD FILLING
500g white fish fillets
½ cup dry white wine
1¼ cups coconut cream, approximately
60g butter
2 onions, chopped
2 tablespoons plain flour
2 teaspoons curry powder
105g can smoked oysters, drained
½ cup cream

Lemon Saffron Crepes: Sift flour into bowl, make well in centre; gradually stir in combined remaining ingredients; beat until smooth. (Or make batter in blender or processor.) Pour 2 to 3 tablespoons batter evenly into heated greased pan; cook until golden brown. Turn Crepe, cook other side. Repeat with remaining batter.

Divide Filling between Crepes, roll up. Place Crepes seam-side down in baking dish in single layer, cover, bake in moderate oven 20 minutes, or until heated through. Reheat remaining coconut mixture, add cream, pour over Crepes before serving.

Seafood Filling: Cut fish into chunks, place in pan with wine, bring to the boil, reduce heat, simmer few minutes, uncovered, until just tender; drain, reserve liquid. Add enough coconut cream to reserved cooking liquid to make up to 2 cups liquid.

Melt butter in pan, add onions, cook, stirring, few minutes until soft and lightly browned. Stir in flour and curry powder, cook 1 minute. Stir in coconut cream mixture, stir constantly over heat until mixture boils and thickens. Combine 1 cup of the coconut cream mixture with fish and the halved oysters.

Serves 4.

MEXICAN MARINATED FISH SALAD IN AVOCADO

This is our version of a raw fish dish popular in Mexico. There is no cooking process, but the marinating makes the fish taste and appear to be cooked.

250g white fish fillets
1 clove garlic, crushed
½ cup lemon juice
1 red pepper, finely chopped
1 tomato, peeled, chopped
1 small red onion, finely chopped
½ cup stuffed green olives, chopped
3 avocados, halved
DRESSING
¼ cup lemon juice
2 tablespoons oil
1 clove garlic, crushed
1 small fresh red chilli, finely chopped
1 teaspoon sugar

Cut fish into small cubes. Combine fish in bowl with garlic and lemon juice, cover, refrigerate overnight. Next day, drain fish well, discard lemon mixture. Combine fish with pepper, tomato, onion, olives and Dressing. Serve fish mixture in avocado halves.

Dressing: Combine all ingredients.

Serves 6.

ABOVE: Mexican Marinated Fish Salad in Avocado.
RIGHT: Back: Scallop-Filled Crepe Baskets; front: Lemon Saffron Crepes with Seafood Filling.

SCALLOP-FILLED CREPE BASKETS

CREPES
½ cup plain flour
2 eggs, lightly beaten
¾ cup milk
1 teaspoon melted butter
FILLING
750g scallops
2 cups water
30g butter
1 clove garlic, crushed
2 tablespoons plain flour
1 teaspoon dry mustard
¾ cup cream
2 egg yolks, lightly beaten
1 tablespoon lemon juice
TOPPING
15g butter
½ cup stale breadcrumbs
1 tablespoon chopped chives
1 teaspoon grated lemon rind

Crepes: Sift flour into bowl, make well in centre, gradually stir in combined eggs, milk and butter, mix to a smooth batter. (Or blend or process mixture until smooth.) Pour 2 to 3 tablespoons of mixture into heated, greased pan; cook until set and lightly browned underneath. Turn Crepes, brown on other side. Repeat with remaining batter. Grease the outside of 6 small ovenproof moulds. Place the inverted moulds onto lightly greased oven tray. Place a Crepe over each mould, bake in moderate oven 10 minutes. When cold, remove Crepes from moulds,

OYSTERS WITH THREE TOPPINGS

Oysters are always a favorite; they are delicious simply served in their shells on a bed of ice accompanied by buttered bread, lemon wedges and freshly ground black pepper. For those who like their oysters dressed up, here are different ways of serving them.

The recipes for Basil Butter and the Toppings will be enough for 12 oysters. Adapt the quantities to suit yourself; you might like to make only one or all three of the Toppings.

3 dozen oysters in shell
BASIL BUTTER
60g butter
2 tablespoons chopped fresh basil
2 tablespoons grated parmesan cheese
1 clove garlic, crushed
¼ cup grated parmesan cheese, extra
BACON AND TOMATO TOPPING
2 bacon rashers, finely chopped
2 tablespoons tomato paste
1 tablespoon vodka
1 teaspoon Worcestershire sauce
SOUR CREAM TOPPING
30g butter
1 tablespoon oil
1 clove garlic, crushed
1 cup stale breadcrumbs
½ cup sour cream
¼ cup grated mozzarella cheese
2 teaspoons lemon juice

Basil Butter: Have butter at room temperature. Beat butter in bowl until smooth, stir in basil, cheese and garlic. Divide over 12 oysters, top with extra cheese, grill until butter is melted.

Bacon and Tomato Topping: Combine bacon, tomato paste, vodka and Worcestershire sauce in bowl, divide over 12 oysters, grill until bacon is crisp and golden brown.

Sour Cream Topping: Heat butter, oil and garlic in pan, add crumbs, stir constantly over heat until golden brown. Combine sour cream, cheese and lemon juice in bowl, divide over 12 oysters, sprinkle with crumbs, grill oysters until Topping is crisp.

Serves 6.

ABOVE: Oysters with Three Toppings; from left: Basil Butter; Sour Cream Topping; Bacon and Tomato Topping. RIGHT: Coconut King Prawns with Curry Sauce.

COCONUT KING PRAWNS WITH CURRY SAUCE

1kg green king prawns
cornflour
½ cup self-raising flour
⅓ cup water
¼ cup coconut cream
1 egg, lightly beaten
¾ cup shredded coconut
oil for deep frying
CURRY SAUCE
1 tablespoon oil
1 clove garlic, crushed
1 tablespoon curry powder
1 tablespoon sugar
2 teaspoons cornflour
¾ cup chicken stock
½ cup coconut cream
2 tablespoons cream
2 tablespoons lemon juice

Shell and devein prawns. Toss prawns in cornflour, shake off excess cornflour. Sift flour into a bowl, make well in centre, gradually stir in combined water, coconut cream and egg; beat until smooth, stir in coconut.

Dip prawns in batter; deep fry prawns, a few at a time, in hot oil until golden brown. Serve with Sauce.

Curry Sauce: Heat oil and garlic in pan, add curry powder and sugar, stir over heat 1 minute. Blend cornflour with a little of the chicken stock, add to pan with remaining stock and coconut cream, stir constantly over heat until mixture boils and thickens. Stir in cream and lemon juice, reheat.

Serves 6.

SEAFOOD MAIN COURSES

Seafood can be as sumptuous or as deliciously simple as you choose; humble sea fare has developed exciting new possibilities since the days when fish and chips were a staple diet. With clever planning, main course seafood need not be excessively expensive. Lobster, Balmain bugs and crab may be food for celebration but less feted fare — fish fillets, squid, sardines — comes into its own with innovative sauces or when served with pasta, or as main ingredients in salads and terrines. For summer entertaining, seafood is a clever choice.

PAN-FRIED TROUT WITH JULIENNE OF VEGETABLES

2 trout
plain flour
1 carrot
1 zucchini
1 stick celery
30g butter
1 tablespoon oil
1 teaspoon dried tarragon leaves
1 teaspoon grated lemon rind
¼ cup brandy
2 teaspoons cornflour
¼ cup cream
¾ cup water

Rub trout all over with flour. Cut carrot, zucchini and celery into thin strips. Heat butter and oil in large pan, add trout, cook until brown on both sides. Add tarragon and lemon rind, cook until trout are just tender. Place trout onto serving plates; keep warm. Add brandy to pan juices, boil until most of the brandy is evaporated, stir in blended cornflour and cream with water to pan, stir constantly over heat until sauce boils and thickens. Boil, steam or microwave vegetables until just tender, drain; serve over trout with sauce.
Serves 2.

POACHED TROUT WITH GINGER WINE SAUCE

4 trout
4 green shallots
2 x 5cm pieces fresh ginger, peeled
¼ cup green ginger wine
¼ cup dry white wine
2 tablespoons lemon juice
90g butter

Place trout in ovenproof dish in single layer, cover with water, bake covered in moderate oven for about 20 minutes or until fish are just tender (or microwave on HIGH for about 5 minutes). Cut shallots and ginger into thin strips about 5cm long.

Combine ginger wine, wine and lemon juice in pan, bring to the boil, boil until reduced to about half. Reduce heat until mixture is just simmering, gradually add small pieces of cold butter, whisking constantly after each addition. Drain trout, place on serving plates, carefully peel away skin. Sprinkle trout with shallots and ginger; top with sauce.

Serves 4.

Clockwise from right: Pan-Fried Trout with Julienne of Vegetables; Fish and Spinach Rolls with Lemon Butter Sauce; Poached Trout with Ginger Wine Sauce; Fish with Balmain Bugs and Creamy Wine Sauce.

FISH WITH BALMAIN BUGS AND CREAMY WINE SAUCE

We used snapper fillets in this recipe. Sliced cooked lobster can be used instead of Balmain bugs if preferred.

6 large white fish fillets
6 cooked Balmain (or Moreton Bay) bugs
CREAMY WINE SAUCE
30g butter
1 small onion, finely chopped
¾ cup dry white wine
¾ cup cream
tiny pinch saffron powder
2 teaspoons lemon juice
1 tablespoon chopped fresh dill

Cut shells away from underside of Balmain bug tails, remove flesh from shells, slice flesh thinly. Pan-fry or grill fish fillets until tender, place onto serving plates, top with Balmain bug slices and Sauce; serve immediately.

Creamy Wine Sauce: Heat butter in pan, add onion, cook, stirring, until onion is soft. Add wine to pan, bring to the boil, boil until wine is reduced by about two-thirds. Add cream to pan, boil until mixture is reduced by half. Stir in saffron, lemon juice and dill.

Serves 6.

FISH AND SPINACH ROLLS WITH LEMON BUTTER SAUCE

We used John Dory in this recipe.

1kg thin white fish fillets
1 bunch English spinach
3 bacon rashers, finely chopped
125g baby mushrooms, thinly sliced
LEMON BUTTER SAUCE
90g butter
¼ cup lemon juice
3 egg yolks
300ml carton cream
1 teaspoon dry mustard

Remove bones from fish. Cover each fillet with spinach. Cook bacon in pan until just crisp, add mushrooms, cook, stirring, few minutes or until mushrooms are tender. Top spinach with mushroom mixture. Roll up fillets to enclose filling, secure with toothpicks. Place in single layer in ovenproof dish, cover and bake in moderate oven 20 minutes or until fish is tender (or microwave on HIGH about 8 minutes). Top sliced fish with hot Sauce; serve immediately.

Lemon Butter Sauce: Melt butter in pan, whisk in combined lemon juice, egg yolks, cream and mustard, whisk constantly over low heat until Sauce thickens slightly; do not allow to boil; serve immediately.

Serves 6.

QUICK 'N' EASY BOUILLABAISSE FOR TWO

Serve this scrumptious soup with crusty bread; cook as close to serving time as possible.

1 small green lobster tail
500g mussels
250g green king prawns
2 cups water
⅔ cup dry white wine
1 tablespoon oil
1 clove garlic, crushed
1 onion, sliced
400g can tomatoes
2 tablespoons tomato paste
1 tablespoon Worcestershire sauce
½ teaspoon tabasco sauce
2 teaspoons sugar
tiny pinch saffron powder
2 tablespoons chopped parsley

Cut lobster tail in half lengthways, leaving shell intact, then cut into 2.5cm pieces (still with shell on). Scrub mussels, remove beard. Shell and devein prawns, leaving tails intact. Combine water and wine in pan, bring to the boil, add seafood, cover, simmer 5 minutes, drain; reserve 1 cup of the stock.

Heat oil in pan, add garlic and onion, cook, stirring, until onion is soft. Add reserved stock, undrained crushed tomatoes, tomato paste, sauces, sugar and saffron to pan. Bring to the boil, cover, reduce heat, simmer 5 minutes; add seafood, heat through gently. Serve immediately in bowls, sprinkled with parsley.

Serves 2.

SEAFOOD AND VEGETABLE PLATTER WITH TWO SAUCES

We used the hot Asian variety of chilli sauce in this recipe.

1kg cooked prawns
500g squid
2 dozen oysters on shell
1 tablespoon oil
1 tablespoon light soy sauce
1 teaspoon chilli sauce
250g broccoli
250g snow peas
2 cucumbers
BASIL AIOLI
4 cloves garlic, crushed
2 egg yolks
1 cup basil leaves
1 cup oil
2 tablespoons lemon juice
GINGER LEMON SAUCE
¼ cup lemon juice
¼ cup oil
2 tablespoons dry white wine
1 tablespoon grated fresh ginger
2 teaspoons light soy sauce
1 teaspoon sugar

Shell and devein prawns, leave tails intact; cut squid into 5cm strips, mark one side of each strip with a diamond pattern. Heat oil in large pan, add squid, soy and chilli sauces, stir-fry few minutes, until squid is tender; cool.

Trim broccoli, cut into flowerets, boil, steam or microwave until just tender. Top and tail snow peas, boil, steam or microwave for 1 minute or until just tender. Peel cucumbers, cut into thin 5cm lengths. Place prawns, squid, oysters, and vegetables on plate. Serve with Aioli and Sauce.

Basil Aioli: Blend or process garlic and egg yolks until smooth, add basil and one-third of the oil, process until smooth, gradually add remaining oil in a thin stream while motor is operating until mixture is thick; add lemon juice, process until smooth.

Ginger Lemon Sauce: Combine all ingredients in jar; shake well.

Serves 6.

RIGHT: Seafood and Vegetable Platter with Two Sauces.
BELOW: Quick 'n' Easy Bouillabaise for Two.

SMOKED FISH AND RICE SLICE

We used smoked cod in this recipe.

500g smoked fish
1 litre (4 cups) chicken stock
2 teaspoons curry powder
1 cup long grain rice
1 egg, lightly beaten
2 eggs, lightly beaten, extra
¾ cup milk
¾ cup cream
1 cup grated tasty cheese
4 green shallots, chopped
1 teaspoon dry mustard
2 tablespoons chopped parsley

Bring stock to the boil in large pan, add curry powder and rice, reduce heat, simmer, covered, for about 30 minutes, or until all liquid has been absorbed and rice is tender; stir in egg. Spread rice mixture evenly over base of greased lamington tin (base measures 16cm x 26cm). Cook fish in pan of simmering water for about 5 minutes, drain, flake with fork, spread over rice. Pour over combined extra eggs, milk, cream, cheese, shallots, mustard and parsley. Bake in moderate oven 30 minutes or until golden brown and set (or microwave on MEDIUM for about 15 minutes or until set). Stand 5 minutes before serving.

Serves 4 to 6.

LOBSTER AND ASPARAGUS WITH ORANGE BUTTER SAUCE

3 green lobster tails
250g snow peas
2 x 250g bunches asparagus
30g butter
4 green shallots, chopped
2 teaspoons grated orange rind
½ cup orange juice
½ cup pine nuts

Cut lobster tails along each side of the underside with scissors, remove skin. Pull lobster flesh away from shells, cut flesh into slices. Top and tail snow peas. Peel and trim asparagus, cut in half, boil, steam or microwave until asparagus is just tender. Add snow peas, cook 1 minute, drain, rinse asparagus, snow peas under cold water; drain.

Heat butter in pan, add shallots, orange rind and juice, add lobster, stir-fry until lobster is just tender, add pine nuts, asparagus and snow peas, stir-fry until heated through.

Serves 4.

SEAFOOD KEBABS WITH CURRIED HONEY GLAZE

Prepare up to 12 hours in advance; keep refrigerated. Grill or barbecue kebabs just before serving. We used ling fish fillets in this recipe.

1kg thick fish fillets
500g scallops
1kg green king prawns
4 zucchini
2 red peppers
CURRIED HONEY GLAZE
60g butter
¼ cup honey
2 teaspoons curry powder
2 teaspoons light soy sauce
SAFFRON RICE
15g butter
1 onion, chopped
2 cups long grain rice
6 cups chicken stock
tiny pinch saffron powder

Cut fish into cubes, trim scallops, peel and devein prawns, leaving tails intact. Slice zucchini, chop peppers.

Thread fish, scallops, prawns, zucchini and peppers onto about 12 skewers. Brush kebabs all over with hot Glaze, cover, refrigerate until ready to cook. Grill or barbecue kebabs over high heat for a few minutes on each side, or until tender. Serve on Rice.

Curried Honey Glaze: Heat all ingredients in pan until butter is melted.

Saffron Rice: Heat butter in large pan, add onion, cook, stirring, until onion is soft, add rice, stock and saffron, bring to the boil, reduce heat; simmer covered for about 30 minutes or until all liquid is absorbed and rice is tender.

Serves 6.

ABOVE: From left: Smoked Fish and Rice Slice; Seafood Kebabs with Curried Honey Glaze.
LEFT: Lobster and Asparagus with Orange Butter Sauce.

LAYERED FISH AND SMOKED SALMON TERRINE

Have all ingredients and equipment well chilled before use. It is necessary to refrigerate the mixture after each step to stop the mixture breaking down during the cooking process.

500g white fish fillets
2 egg whites
1 egg
1 teaspoon grated lemon rind
1 tablespoon lemon juice
few drops tabasco sauce
2 x 300ml cartons cream
125g sliced smoked salmon

Roughly chop boned fish fillets. Blend or process fish until smooth, add egg whites, egg, lemon rind and juice and tabasco; process until smooth. Refrigerate mixture in processor bowl for 10 minutes. Return bowl to processor. With motor operating, pour in half the cream in a thin stream, refrigerate 10 minutes. Add remaining cream, refrigerate 10 minutes. Pour half the mixture into a greased ovenproof dish (base measures 9cm x 22cm), top with salmon slices, then remaining fish mixture. Cover dish with greased foil, place dish in baking dish with enough hot water to come about two-thirds of the way up sides of dish. Bake in moderate oven 1 hour, cool Terrine to room temperature, refrigerate 1 hour, then cut into slices to serve.

Serves 6.

FETTUCINE WITH CREAMY SMOKED SALMON SAUCE

We used fresh pasta, which takes about three minutes to cook, dried pasta will take at least 10 minutes.

10 slices (about 300g) smoked
    salmon
750g fettucine
250g snow peas
15g butter
1 onion, finely chopped
¼ cup dry white wine
⅔ cup cream
1 teaspoon tomato paste
1 egg, lightly beaten

Cut smoked salmon into strips. Add pasta to large pan of rapidly boiling water, boil until just tender; drain. Top and tail snow peas. Melt butter in large pan, add onion and snow peas, stir-fry until onion is soft. Add wine, bring to the boil, reduce heat, stir in combined cream, tomato paste and egg. Stir in fettucine and salmon, heat thoroughly; serve immediately.

Serves 6.

COLD SQUID SALAD PROVENCALE

Make up to one day ahead if desired.

1kg small squid, sliced
15g butter
1 tablespoon olive oil
1 onion, finely chopped
400g can tomatoes
1 red pepper, finely chopped
1 clove garlic, crushed
½ cup dry white wine
1 tablespoon tomato paste
½ teaspoon dried oregano leaves
4 pitted black olives, chopped
¼ cup fresh basil leaves

Bring a pan of water to the boil, add squid, return water to the boil, drain immediately; refrigerate squid while making sauce.

Heat butter and oil in pan, add onion, cook, stirring, until onion is soft, add crushed undrained tomatoes, pepper, garlic, wine, tomato paste and oregano, bring to the boil, reduce heat; simmer 10 minutes. Blend or process tomato sauce mixture until smooth. Pour into bowl, stir in olives and squid, mix well; refrigerate before serving. Serve topped with sliced basil leaves.

Serves 4.

SCALLOP AND BROWN RICE SALAD WITH TANGY DRESSING

750g scallops
1 cup dry white wine
½ cup water
⅔ cup brown rice
2 sticks celery
1 red pepper
250g baby mushrooms, sliced
TANGY DRESSING
½ cup French dressing
1 tablespoon lemon juice
1 teaspoon seeded mustard

Combine wine and water in pan, bring to the boil, add scallops, return to the boil; drain. Rinse scallops under cold water, drain. Add rice gradually to large pan of boiling water, boil rapidly uncovered 30 minutes or until just tender. Drain, rinse under cold water, drain. Cut celery and pepper into thin strips about 5cm long. Combine scallops, rice, mushrooms, celery, pepper and Dressing just before serving.

Tangy Dressing: Combine all ingredients in jar; shake well.

Serves 6.

Back from left: Fettucine with Creamy Smoked Salmon Sauce; Scallop and Brown Rice Salad with Tangy Dressing; front, from left: Cold Squid Salad Provencale; Layered Fish and Smoked Salmon Terrine.

SALMON-SEASONED FISH FILLETS

We used bream fillets in this recipe. Prepare for baking up to 12 hours beforehand if preferred.

6 thin white fish fillets
440g can red salmon, drained
30g butter
1 onion, chopped
1 stick celery, chopped
1 teaspoon grated lemon rind
1 tablespoon lemon juice
1 teaspoon chopped fresh dill
½ cup cream
2 teaspoons light soy sauce
2 tablespoons chopped parsley

Remove skin and bones from fish. Melt butter in pan, add onion and celery, cook, stirring, until onion is soft (or microwave on HIGH for about 5 minutes). Remove from heat, stir in lemon rind and juice, dill and flaked salmon. Press mixture evenly onto skin side of each fish fillet, fold fillets in half to enclose mixture; secure with toothpicks. Place fish into greased ovenproof dish in single layer, pour over combined cream and soy sauce, cover, bake in moderate oven 20 minutes or until fish is just tender (or microwave on HIGH for about 7 minutes). Serve fish topped with cream mixture from pan, sprinkle with parsley.

Serves 6.

FISH FILLETS WITH CITRUS SAUCE

We used snapper fillets in this recipe.

4 large white fish fillets
plain flour
30g butter
1 tablespoon oil
2 tablespoons lemon juice
½ cup grated tasty cheese
CITRUS SAUCE
300ml carton thickened cream
1 tablespoon dry sherry
2 tablespoons dry white wine
1 teaspoon grated orange rind
1 teaspoon grated lemon rind
2 tablespoons lemon juice
2 egg yolks, lightly beaten

Remove skin and bones from fish, rub both sides of fish with flour. Heat butter and oil in large pan, add fish, cook on both sides until browned, add lemon juice, cook further few minutes or until fish is just tender. Place fish on serving plates, top with Sauce, sprinkle with cheese, grill a few minutes or until cheese is melted; serve immediately.

Citrus Sauce: Combine cream, sherry, wine, orange and lemon rinds and lemon juice in pan, bring to the boil, reduce heat, simmer uncovered for about 10 minutes. Remove from heat, quickly stir in egg yolks, stir until sauce is slightly thickened; use immediately.

Serves 4.

CRUMB-TOPPED GARFISH WITH SAMBUCCA

Sambucca is a delicious aniseed-flavored liqueur. Pernod or Ouzo could be substituted if preferred.

1kg garfish
½ cup lemon juice
½ cup dry white wine
¼ cup Sambucca
¼ cup oil
1 tablespoon chopped fresh dill
60g butter
2 tablespoons oil, extra
plain flour
¼ cup Sambucca, extra
2 tablespoons chopped fresh dill, extra
CRUMB TOPPING
30g butter
1 cup stale breadcrumbs
2 green shallots, chopped

Clean fish, drain on absorbent paper. Combine lemon juice, white wine, Sambucca, oil and dill in bowl, add fish, cover, marinate several hours or overnight. Drain fish; reserve 1 cup of the marinade. Heat butter and extra oil in large pan, toss fish in flour, cook for about 2 minutes on each side or until fish are tender. Heat reserved marinade in pan, add extra Sambucca, flame, cook, stirring 1 minute, add extra dill. Spoon over fish, sprinkle with Topping; serve immediately.

Crumb Topping: Heat butter in pan, add crumbs and shallots, cook, stirring, until crumbs are golden brown.

Serves 6.

CRUMBED SARDINES WITH TOMATO AND CAPER SAUCE

1kg sardines
½ cup oil
2 tablespoons chopped capers
2 eggs, lightly beaten
1½ cups dry breadcrumbs
1 cup grated parmesan cheese
oil for shallow frying
TOMATO AND CAPER SAUCE
2 tablespoons oil
1 clove garlic, crushed
1 small onion, chopped
400g can tomatoes
2 tablespoons capers
½ cup halved black olives

LEFT: From left: Salmon-Seasoned Fish Fillets; Fish Fillets with Citrus Sauce.
BELOW: From left: Crumbed Sardines with Tomato and Caper Sauce; Crumb-Topped Garfish with Sambucca.

STEP 1
Cut heads from fish, cut underpart of fish open, gently press backbones away with thumbs, as shown.

STEP 2
Gently pull backbones away from flesh. Wash and drain fish well, combine with oil and capers, cover, marinate several hours or overnight. Drain fish; discard marinade. Dip fish into eggs, then combined crumbs and cheese. Heat oil

for shallow frying in large pan, add fish, fry each side for about 2 minutes or until fish are just tender and golden brown. Serve with Sauce.

Tomato and Caper Sauce: Heat oil in pan, add garlic and onion, cook 2 minutes, stirring, until onion is soft. Add undrained crushed tomatoes, bring to the boil, reduce heat, simmer 30 minutes or until Sauce is reduced to about half; add capers and olives.

Serves 6.

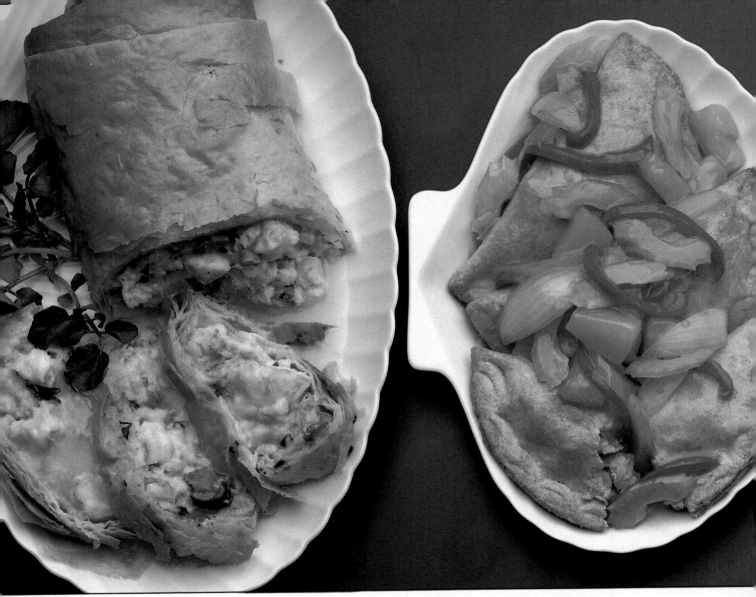

SMOKED FISH TURNOVERS WITH SWEET AND SOUR SAUCE

We used haddock in this recipe.

750g smoked fish
1 egg, lightly beaten
2 teaspoons lemon juice
900g packet wholemeal pastry
 sheets
1 egg, lightly beaten, extra
SWEET AND SOUR SAUCE
1 tablespoon oil
1 onion, chopped
1 red pepper, chopped
1 stick celery, chopped
450g can pineapple pieces
2 tablespoons arrowroot
½ cup white vinegar
3 teaspoons tomato sauce
2 teaspoons light soy sauce
2 teaspoons grated fresh ginger
2 tablespoons sugar
1 chicken stock cube

Poach, steam or microwave fish until tender; drain, flake, remove bones. Combine fish with egg and lemon juice. Cut pastry into 12 x 14cm rounds. Place a tablespoonful of the fish mixture in centre of each round, glaze edges with extra egg, fold in half, press edges together firmly. Place turnovers onto lightly greased oven trays, brush with egg, bake in moderately hot oven 20 minutes or until golden brown. Serve hot Turnovers with Sauce.

Sweet and Sour Sauce: Heat oil in pan, add onion, pepper and celery, cook, stirring, until onion is soft; remove from pan. Drain pineapple, reserve syrup. Blend arrowroot with a little of the vinegar until smooth, measure reserved pineapple syrup, add enough water to measure 1 cup. Add arrowroot mixture, remaining vinegar, tomato sauce, soy sauce, ginger, sugar, crumbled stock cube and reserved syrup to pan, stir constantly over heat until mixture boils and thickens. Return vegetable mixture to pan, reheat, serve immediately.

Makes 12.

SCALLOP PUFFS WITH RATATOUILLE SAUCE

Puffs can be cooked a day before required; filling should be made as close to serving time as possible. Reheat Puffs in moderate oven uncovered on oven tray for about 10 minutes.

1kg scallops
125g prosciutto, chopped
750g packet ready rolled puff
 pastry
1 egg, lightly beaten
1 small eggplant, sliced
1 litre (4 cups) water
30g butter
1 onion, finely chopped
3 zucchini, finely chopped
1 red pepper, finely chopped
1 clove garlic, crushed
2 tomatoes, peeled, seeded
¼ cup dry white wine
1 tablespoon tomato paste
300ml carton cream

SEAFOOD AND CHEESE STRUDELS WITH LEMON SAUCE

Prepare Strudels up to a day ahead if preferred. Keep covered in refrigerator. We used ling fish in this recipe. Mussel meat can be bought fresh or frozen from specialist fish shops.

500g white fish fillets, chopped
1kg cooked prawns, shelled
250g mussel meat, chopped
½ cup grated tasty cheese
60g butter
¾ cup plain flour
1 cup milk
300g carton sour cream
10 green shallots, chopped
¼ cup lemon juice
375g packet fillo pastry
250g butter, melted, extra
¾ cup dry breadcrumbs
¾ cup grated parmesan cheese
2 tablespoons chopped parsley
1 teaspoon dry mustard
LEMON SAUCE
60g butter
1 clove garlic, crushed
1½ tablespoons cornflour
2 cups water
2 tablespoons lemon juice
1 teaspoon grated lemon rind
tiny pinch saffron powder

Add fish to pan of cold water, bring to the boil, reduce heat, cover, simmer few minutes or until fish is just tender. Remove fish from pan, combine in bowl with chopped prawns, mussels and tasty cheese.

Melt butter in pan, add flour, stir until smooth, cook, stirring, for 1 minute. Gradually stir in milk and sour cream, stir constantly over heat until mixture boils and thickens, remove from heat, stir in shallots and lemon juice, stir in seafood mixture; cool to room temperature.

Brush a sheet of pastry with extra butter, top with another sheet of pastry, brush with butter; sprinkle with about a tablespoon of the combined breadcrumbs, parmesan cheese, parsley and mustard. Repeat buttering between each layer of pastry and sprinkling with breadcrumb mixture between every second layer, until half the pastry has been used. Place half the seafood mixture along the long side of the pastry, leaving a 5cm border. Fold sides in, roll up like a Swiss roll. Brush all over with butter. Repeat with remaining ingredients to make another strudel. Place strudels onto a large oven tray. Bake in moderate oven for 30 minutes. Serve hot with Sauce.

Lemon Sauce: Heat butter and garlic in pan, stir in blended cornflour and water, lemon juice, lemon rind and saffron; stir constantly over heat until mixture boils and thickens.

Serves 8.

Cut pastry sheets into 8 x 13cm rounds, place 4 rounds onto oven trays. Cut 1.5cm rings from the remaining 4 rounds of pastry and place on the 4 larger circles to make a raised edge. Place smaller rounds onto oven trays. Brush all rounds of pastry with egg, bake in moderately hot oven 15 minutes, change position of oven trays half way through cooking time.

Spread eggplant out onto wire rack, sprinkle with salt on both sides, stand 20 minutes. Rinse eggplant under cold water, dry well, then chop finely. Clean and trim scallops. Place water in pan, bring to the boil, add scallops, return water to the boil, remove scallops from pan, drain well; reserve 1 cup of the cooking liquid.

Heat butter in pan, add onion, cook, stirring, until onion is soft, add eggplant, zucchini, pepper, garlic, finely chopped tomatoes, wine, tomato paste and the reserved stock. Bring to the boil, reduce heat, simmer 15 minutes. Add cream, simmer further 5 minutes. Just before pastry is cooked add scallops and prosciutto to sauce, heat through gently; serve immediately in pastry cases.

Serves 4.

From left: Seafood and Cheese Strudels with Lemon Sauce; Smoked Fish Turnovers with Sweet and Sour Sauce; Scallop Puffs with Ratatouille Sauce.

PAN-FRIED SEASONED BACON-WRAPPED FISH

We used large snapper cutlets in this recipe. Fish can be prepared and frozen for up to a month if desired.

4 white fish steaks or cutlets
4 bacon rashers
30g butter
SEASONING
½ cup grated tasty cheese
1 cup stale breadcrumbs
4 green shallots, chopped
1 tablespoon tomato sauce

Press Seasoning between tail ends of fish cutlets. Wrap bacon around ends of cutlets to enclose Seasoning, secure with toothpicks. Melt butter in large pan, add cutlets, gently fry on both sides until tender (or microwave on HIGH for about 6 minutes, turning once during cooking).
Seasoning: Combine all ingredients.
Serves 4.

FISH AND SPINACH IN CHEESE SAUCE WITH CRUNCHY TOPPING

We used gemfish in this recipe.

1kg thick white fish fillets
30g butter, melted
2 tablespoons lemon juice
1 tablespoon oil
1 clove garlic, crushed
2 bunches English spinach
60g butter, extra
½ cup plain flour
2 cups milk
300g carton sour cream
125g blue cheese
CRUNCHY TOPPING
30g butter
2 tablespoons oil
1½ cups stale breadcrumbs
½ cup grated parmesan cheese

Place fish in pan, cover with water, bring to the boil, reduce heat, simmer uncovered for a few minutes or until just tender; drain well. Lightly flake fish into bowl, add butter and lemon juice.

Heat oil and garlic in pan add spinach leaves, cook, stirring, for a few minutes or until spinach is just wilted; stir into fish mixture. Heat extra butter in pan, add flour, cook, stirring, 1 minute, gradually stir in milk, stir until sauce boils and thickens. Blend or process sour cream and cheese until smooth, stir into sauce, stir gently into fish mixture, spread into greased ovenproof dish; sprinkle with Topping. Bake in moderate oven 30 minutes or until golden brown.
Crunchy Topping: Melt butter and oil in pan, add breadcrumbs, cook, stirring, until crumbs are golden brown; stir in cheese.
Serves 6.

CHILLED FISH STEAKS WITH PRAWN MAYONNAISE

We used jewfish cutlets in this recipe.

4 white fish cutlets or steaks
60g butter
2 tablespoons lemon juice
1 tablespoon chopped parsley
PRAWN MAYONNAISE
500g cooked prawns, shelled
1 egg yolk
1 tablespoon white vinegar
1 teaspoon grated lemon rind
2 teaspoons lemon juice
2 teaspoons tomato sauce
½ cup oil

Heat butter and lemon juice in large pan, add fish, fry gently on both sides until just tender (or microwave on HIGH for about 4 minutes), remove from pan, drain on absorbent paper till cool, refrigerate until cold. Serve fish with Mayonnaise and parsley garnish.
Prawn Mayonnaise: Blend or process prawns with egg yolk, vinegar, lemon rind and juice and tomato sauce until smooth. Gradually add oil in thin stream while motor is operating; blend until Mayonnaise is smooth and thick.
Serves 4.

PEPPERED FISH WITH LIME BUTTER

We used salmon steaks in this recipe.

6 white fish steaks or cutlets
2 tablespoons oil
⅓ cup dried green peppercorns
60g butter
1 tablespoon oil, extra
LIME BUTTER
125g butter
2 teaspoons grated lime rind
2 tablespoons lime juice
1 clove garlic, crushed

Brush fish steaks with oil, crush peppercorns in blender, coat each side of the steaks with peppercorns. Heat butter and extra oil in large pan, add fish, pan-fry each side for a few minutes, then cook until fish is just tender (or microwave on HIGH for about 4 minutes). Serve with slices of Lime Butter.
Lime Butter: Have butter at room temperature, combine with remaining ingredients. Place Butter onto a piece of greaseproof paper shape into a log. Wrap in foil, refrigerate until firm.
Serves 6.

Clockwise from front right: Chilled Fish Steaks with Prawn Mayonnaise; Peppered Fish with Lime Butter; Pan-Fried Seasoned Bacon-Wrapped Fish; Fish and Spinach in Cheese Sauce with Crunchy Topping.

PEPPERED KING PRAWNS

Pimientos are available in jars or cans; they are an imported product available from delicatessens.

1½kg green king prawns
185g can pimientos, drained
2 tablespoons dried green peppercorns
2 tablespoons dried black peppercorns
1 tablespoon coriander seeds
2 tablespoons oil
60g butter
2 cloves garlic, crushed
2 tablespoons brandy
1 teaspoon sugar

Shell and devein prawns, leaving tails intact. Slice pimientos finely. Crush peppercorns and coriander in blender.

Heat oil and butter in large pan, add garlic and peppercorn mixture, cook, stirring, 2 minutes, add prawns, cook, stirring, for about 4 minutes or until prawns are just tender, stir in pimientos. Place prawn mixture onto serving plates, add brandy and sugar to pan, flame, cook, stirring, 1 minute; pour over prawns; serve immediately.
Serves 6.

FISH ROLLS WITH ASPARAGUS HOLLANDAISE SAUCE

Prepare fish rolls ready for baking up to 12 hours ahead if preferred. We used bream fillets in this recipe.

6 thin white fish fillets
3 bacon rashers, chopped
250g bunch asparagus, chopped
1 cup grated tasty cheese
15g butter, melted
ASPARAGUS HOLLANDAISE
250g bunch asparagus, chopped
4 egg yolks
1 tablespoon lemon juice
125g butter, melted

Remove skin and bones from fish, poach, steam or microwave fish until just tender, drain on absorbent paper. Cook bacon in pan until crisp, drain on absorbent paper. Combine asparagus, cheese and bacon in bowl, press mixture onto the skin side of each fillet, roll up, place in greased ovenproof dish in single layer. Brush with butter, cover with greaseproof paper, bake in moderate oven 20 minutes (or microwave on HIGH for about 8 minutes) or until filling is cooked through. Serve with Asparagus Hollandaise.

Asparagus Hollandaise: Boil, steam or microwave asparagus until tender, blend or process egg yolks and lemon juice until smooth, add hot bubbly butter gradually while motor is operating. Add hot asparagus, process until smooth, serve immediately.
Serves 6.

PRAWNS WITH PERNOD AND ALMOND AND CHIVE RICE

You will need to cook two-thirds cup rice for this recipe. Pernod is an aniseed-flavored liqueur. Sambucca or Ouzo can be substituted.

1kg green prawns
15g butter
1 onion, finely chopped
1 clove garlic, crushed
1 fennel bulb, sliced
2 x 400g cans tomatoes
¼ cup Pernod
¼ cup thickened cream
ALMOND AND CHIVE RICE
2 tablespoons slivered almonds
2 cups cooked rice
15g butter, melted
2 teaspoons finely chopped chives

Peel and devein prawns, leaving tails intact. Heat butter in pan, add onion, cook, stirring, until onion is soft, add garlic, fennel, undrained crushed tomatoes and Pernod. Bring to the boil, reduce heat, simmer uncovered 10 minutes, add cream and prawns, cook about 3 minutes, or until prawns change color; serve with Rice.

Almond and Chive Rice: Toast almonds on oven tray in moderate oven for about 5 minutes. Combine almonds in bowl with rice, butter and chives. Press mixture into 4 individual dishes (½ cup capacity), bake in moderate oven 10 minutes.
Serves 4.

SHALLOT AND GINGER FISH WITH SOY SAUCE

We used ocean perch in this recipe.

4 thick white fish fillets
5cm piece fresh ginger, peeled
3 cups chicken stock
8 green shallots, chopped
1 tablespoon light soy sauce

Cut ginger into thin slices, then into thin strips. Heat stock in pan, add ginger, cook 2 minutes, strain ginger from pan, combine with shallots. Add fish to stock in pan, cover, simmer 5 minutes or until fish is just tender; reserve 2 tablespoons stock. Place fish onto serving plates, top with ginger and shallots. Combine soy sauce with reserved stock in pan, bring to the boil, pour over fish; serve immediately.
Serves 4.

LEFT: Back: Prawns with Pernod and Almond and Chive Rice; front: Peppered King Prawns.
BELOW: Back: Fish Rolls with Asparagus Hollandaise Sauce; front: Shallot and Ginger Fish with Soy Sauce.

MAIN EVENTS

Main courses need not be especially substantial or traditional. We've given variations on pasta dishes, quiches, pizzas and a medley of meat menus. Quick ways with barbecued chicken will be useful for those short-order occasions.

Pasta

SAUCES FOR PASTA

All the Sauces in this section are enough to serve four. The amount of pasta required should be between 250g and 375g depending on whether the dish is to be served as an entree or main course.

The type of pasta you use doesn't matter; there are many flavors, shapes and sizes available to you. Fresh pasta is also readily available.

The cooking time depends on the pasta used: fresh will take three to five minutes, dried up to 15 minutes. Always add pasta gradually to a large pan of rapidly boiling water to which a teaspoon of oil or butter has been added. Boil rapidly uncovered until the pasta is just tender (or al dente). Drain the pasta well, do not rinse, serve it immediately for best results.

FRESH MIXED HERBS AND BLUE CHEESE SAUCE

This delicious Sauce is best made and served immediately to get the most flavor from the fresh herbs. Any fresh herb or combination of fresh herbs can be used in this recipe.

60g butter
1 tablespoon oil
1 clove garlic, crushed
1 onion, finely chopped
2 tablespoons chopped fresh basil
1 tablespoon fresh marjoram leaves
1 tablespoon fresh oregano leaves
125g blue cheese
½ cup grated parmesan cheese
300ml carton cream
1 tablespoon plain flour
½ cup milk
375g pasta

Heat butter and oil in pan, add garlic and onion, cook, stirring, until onion is soft. Add herbs, then crumbled blue cheese, stir until cheese is melted.

Stir in parmesan cheese and cream, then blended flour and milk. Cook, stirring constantly, until mixture boils and thickens. Serve over hot pasta.

Serves 4.

CHILLI BOLOGNAISE SAUCE

Sauce can be made a day before.

500g minced beef
1 tablespoon oil
2 onions, chopped
2 cloves garlic, crushed
400g can tomatoes
1 cup canned tomato puree
½ teaspoon dried oregano leaves
½ teaspoon chilli powder
310g can red kidney beans, drained
125g baby mushrooms, sliced
375g pasta

Heat oil in pan, add onions and garlic, cook, stirring, until onions are soft. Add mince, cook, stirring, until well browned. Add undrained crushed tomatoes, tomato puree, oregano and chilli powder, bring to the boil, reduce heat, simmer uncovered 20 minutes or until Sauce is thick. Add beans and mushrooms, heat thoroughly; serve over hot boiled pasta.

Serves 4.

CREAMY SEAFOOD SAUCE

Smoked salmon off-cuts can be bought quite cheaply at some delicatessens. Make Sauce as close to serving time as possible; seafood will toughen on reheating.

500g green king prawns
250g white fish
125g scallops
60g smoked salmon
30g butter
1 onion, finely chopped
1 cup dry white wine
1 cup water
300ml carton cream
1 tablespoon chopped parsley
1 tablespoon lemon juice
375g pasta

Shell and devein prawns. Remove skin and bones from fish, cut fish into 2cm cubes. Cut salmon into thin strips.

Melt butter in pan, add onion, cook, stirring, until onion is soft. Add wine and water, bring to boil. Add prawns, fish and scallops, return to the boil, simmer few minutes or until tender. Remove seafood from pan, continue to boil wine mixture uncovered, until reduced to about one third. Add cream, bring to the boil, boil uncovered until reduced to about half. Add seafood, salmon, parsley and lemon juice, reheat gently. Serve over hot pasta.

Serves 4.

Back, from left: Creamy Seafood Sauce; Chilli Bolognaise Sauce; front, from left: Tomato and Pimiento Sauce; Fresh Mixed Herbs and Blue Cheese Sauce.

TOMATO AND PIMIENTO SAUCE

Sauce can be made a day before.

1 tablespoon oil
1 clove garlic, crushed
1 kg tomatoes, peeled, chopped
400g can tomatoes
185g can pimientos, drained
3 tablespoons chopped parsley
375g pasta

Heat oil in pan, add garlic, tomatoes, undrained crushed canned tomatoes, chopped pimientos and 2 tablespoons of the parsley, bring to the boil, reduce heat, simmer 30 minutes. Serve over hot pasta with grated parmesan cheese if desired. Sprinkle with remaining parsley just before serving.

Serves 4.

ABOVE: Back, from left: Asparagus Frittata; Watercress and Spinach Roulade with Bacon; front: Mushroom Strudel. RIGHT: Back: Marinara Sauce; front: Tortellini with Creamy Basil and Bacon Sauce.

MARINARA SAUCE

The tomato part of this Sauce can be made a day ahead. Cook the seafood as close to serving time as possible; seafood will toughen on reheating.

250g small squid
750g mussels
500g cooked prawns
2 x 400g cans tomatoes
1 tablespoon oil
1 clove garlic, crushed
1 tablespoon tomato paste
¼ cup dry white wine
375g pasta

Clean squid, cut in half, score inside, cut into squares. Drop squid into pan of boiling water, return to the boil; drain immediately. Wash and scrub mussels, drop into large pan of boiling water, cook few minutes or until mussels open; drain, discard any unopened mussels.

Remove mussel flesh from shells. Shell and devein prawns. Process or blend undrained tomatoes until smooth. Heat oil and garlic in pan, add tomatoes, tomato paste and wine, bring to the boil, reduce heat, simmer uncovered for about 30 minutes or until thick. Add seafood to hot tomato mixture, serve over hot pasta with grated parmesan cheese if desired.

Serves 4.

TORTELLINI WITH CREAMY BASIL AND BACON SAUCE

Sauce can be made up to two hours ahead of serving; cover surface with plastic wrap to exclude air. Tortellini can be bought frozen in delicatessens and supermarkets.

750g tortellini
2 cups fresh basil leaves
300ml carton cream
30g butter
2 bacon rashers, chopped
2 onions, chopped
1 tablespoon lemon juice
¼ cup parmesan cheese

Blend or process basil until finely chopped; add cream, blend until combined. Melt butter in pan, add bacon and onions, cook, stirring, until bacon is crisp. Stir in basil mixture, lemon juice and cheese, heat through. Add tortellini to pan of boiling water, boil rapidly uncovered for about 10 minutes or until tender; drain. Serve immediately with hot basil Sauce.

Serves 6.

Vegetable Features

ASPARAGUS FRITTATA

310g can asparagus spears, drained
2 bacon rashers, chopped
1 large onion, chopped
6 eggs
**2 tablespoons grated parmesan
cheese**
1 teaspoon curry powder

Drain asparagus on absorbent paper, cut spears into 3 pieces. Cook bacon and onion in pan until onion is soft.

Beat eggs, cheese and curry powder together with fork, stir in bacon mixture, pour into greased pie plate (base measures 20cm), top with asparagus. Bake in moderate oven 15 minutes or until set, serve immediately.

WATERCRESS AND SPINACH ROULADE WITH BACON

1 bunch watercress
250g packet frozen spinach
60g butter
⅓ cup plain flour
1 cup milk
⅓ cup grated parmesan cheese
4 eggs, separated
FILLING
4 bacon rashers, finely chopped
1 clove garlic, crushed
185g can pimientos, drained
2 tablespoons chopped fresh basil
250g packet cream cheese
2 tablespoons cream

Chop watercress sprigs finely (or process until coarsely chopped). You should have about 1 cup chopped watercress. Thaw spinach in pan over heat, heat until liquid has evaporated. Heat butter in pan, add flour, cook, stirring, 1 minute, gradually stir in milk, stir constantly over heat until mixture boils and thickens. Stir in cheese, egg yolks, spinach and watercress; transfer mixture to a large bowl.

Beat egg whites until soft peaks form, fold lightly into watercress mixture. Pour mixture into greased and lined Swiss roll tin (base measures 25cm x 30cm). Bake in moderately hot oven for about 20 minutes or until puffed and golden brown. Remove from oven, turn onto wire rack covered with tea towel, carefully remove lining paper; cool to room temperature. Spread with cream cheese mixture then bacon mixture. Use towel to help you roll the Roulade.

Filling: Add bacon and garlic to pan, cook, stirring, until bacon is crisp; stir in sliced pimientos and basil. Have cream cheese at room temperature, beat in small bowl with electric mixer until smooth, stir in cream.

MUSHROOM STRUDEL

You will need to buy a 375g packet fillo pastry, remaining pastry can be sealed and refrigerated for future use.

125g butter
500g baby mushrooms, sliced
1 clove garlic, crushed
⅓ cup plain flour
½ cup milk
⅓ cup sour cream
6 sheets fillo pastry
¼ cup dry breadcrumbs
¼ cup grated parmesan cheese
1 teaspoon dry mustard

Heat 30g of the butter in large pan, add mushrooms and garlic, cook, stirring occasionally, until mushrooms are soft and all liquid evaporated. Melt another 15g of the butter in pan, stir in flour, cook, stirring, for 1 minute. Gradually stir in milk and cream, stir until mixture boils and thickens. Stir in mushrooms; cool to room temperature.

Place one sheet of pastry on bench (cover remaining pastry with grease-proof paper and well wrung-out cloth) brush with some of the remaining melted butter, top with another sheet of pastry, brush with butter, sprinkle with about a tablespoon of the combined breadcrumbs, parmesan cheese and mustard. Repeat buttering and layering until pastry and crumb mixture is used.

Place mushroom mixture along the long side of pastry, leaving a 5cm border. Fold edges of pastry in, roll up. Brush all over with butter. Place on oven tray, bake in moderate oven for about 30 minutes.

Serves 4 to 6.

Pizzas

All the Pizzas in these recipes can be frozen, cooked or uncooked, for up to a month. Reheat frozen cooked Pizzas, covered with foil with holes slashed in top, in moderate oven for about 40 minutes. Or cook frozen uncooked Pizzas, covered in foil in hot oven, for about 20 minutes; reduce heat to moderate, uncover Pizzas, cook for about another 30 minutes. These times are a guide only, all the different bases will need different times. When using dried yeast it is necessary to use reasonably hot water to activate the yeast. Each of these recipes will make two Pizzas.

PANTRY SEAFOOD PIZZA WITH SOFT CRUST
SOFT CRUST
1 teaspoon sugar
7g sachet dried yeast
1⅓ cups hot water
4 cups plain flour
1 teaspoon salt
2 tablespoons oil
TOPPING
1 tablespoon oil
1 onion, chopped
400g can tomatoes
2 tablespoons chopped fresh basil
2 cups (200g) grated mozzarella cheese
200g can shelled prawns, drained
290g can clams, drained
185g can crab, drained
45g can anchovy fillets, drained
2 cups (200g) grated mozzarella cheese
2 tablespoons fresh oregano leaves
Soft Crust: Dissolve sugar and yeast in water in bowl, cover, stand in warm place 10 minutes or until mixture is foamy. Sift flour and salt into large bowl, stir in yeast mixture, then oil. Turn dough onto lightly floured surface, knead for about 10 minutes or until dough is smooth and elastic. Place dough in lightly oiled bowl, cover, stand in warm place for about 45 minutes or until dough has doubled in bulk. Knead dough until smooth, divide in half, roll out large enough to fit 2 greased 28cm pizza pans. Spread dough evenly with tomato mixture, then cheese, then top with seafood mixture and oregano. Bake in moderately hot oven for about 25 minutes or until golden brown.
Topping: Heat oil in pan, add onion, cook, stirring, until onion is soft. Add undrained crushed tomatoes and basil, bring to the boil, reduce heat, simmer uncovered 20 minutes or until thick; cool. Combine all seafood.

PUFF PIZZA WITH THREE-CHEESE TOPPING
2 x 375g packets frozen puff pastry
2 cups (200g) grated mozzarella cheese
150g ricotta cheese
150g gorgonzola cheese
8 canned artichokes, thinly sliced
2 onions, finely sliced
½ cup chopped black olives
Thaw pastry to room temperature. Roll out each packet of pastry large enough to fit a greased 28cm pizza pan. Sprinkle both bases with mozzarella cheese, then crumbled ricotta and gorgonzola. Top with artichokes, onion rings and olives. Bake Pizzas in hot oven 10 minutes, reduce heat to moderately hot, bake further 15 minutes or until puffed and golden brown.

SPINACH AND FETA CHEESE PIZZA WITH WHOLEMEAL CRISPY CRUST
3 bunches English spinach
30g butter
1 onion, chopped
1 clove garlic, crushed
125g feta cheese, chopped
¼ cup tomato paste
3 cups (300g) grated mozzarella cheese
⅓ cup grated parmesan cheese
WHOLEMEAL CRISPY CRUST
1½ cups wholemeal plain flour
1 teaspoon sugar
1 teaspoon salt
7g sachet dried yeast
2 tablespoons oil
½ cup hot water
Divide dough in half, roll out large enough to line 2 greased 28cm pizza pans. Bring a large pan of water to the boil, add spinach leaves, return to the boil, reduce heat, simmer few minutes; drain well, chop spinach roughly, press out as much liquid as possible.

Heat butter in pan, add onion and garlic, cook until onion is soft. Combine spinach in bowl with onion mixture and feta cheese. Spread tomato paste over bases, top with half the mozzarella cheese, then the spinach mixture, top with combined parmesan and remaining mozzarella cheese. Bake Pizzas in moderately hot oven for about 20 minutes.
Wholemeal Crispy Crust: Sift flour, sugar and salt into bowl, add yeast. Make well in centre, add combined oil and water, mix to a firm dough, turn onto floured surface, knead for about 10 minutes or until dough is smooth and elastic. Place in lightly oiled bowl, cover, stand in warm place for about 30 minutes or until dough has doubled in bulk. Knead dough until smooth.

QUICK AND EASY HAM AND PINEAPPLE PIZZA

This Pizza has a scone base which is easy enough for children to prepare. Wholemeal self-raising flour can be substituted for white flour if preferred.

3 cups (300g) grated mozzarella cheese
2 onions, thinly sliced
850g can pineapple pieces, drained
2 green peppers, thinly sliced
375g ham, finely chopped
SCONE DOUGH
2 cups self-raising flour
30g butter
¾ cup milk, approximately
Divide dough in half, roll out large enough to fit 2 greased 28cm pizza pans. Top with cheese, then onions, pineapple, peppers and ham. Bake in hot oven for about 20 minutes or until golden brown.
Scone Dough: Sift flour into bowl, rub in butter, add enough milk to mix to a firm dough. Turn onto lightly floured surface, knead lightly until smooth.

ONION AND PEPPER PIZZA WITH THICK WHOLEMEAL CRUST
45g butter
2 tablespoons oil
4 onions, sliced
2 red peppers, sliced
2 green peppers, sliced
1 clove garlic, crushed
1 teaspoon dried oregano leaves
4 cups (400g) grated mozzarella cheese
1 cup (100g) grated parmesan cheese
THICK WHOLEMEAL CRUST
1 teaspoon sugar
7g sachet dried yeast
1⅓ cups hot water
2 cups wholemeal plain flour
2 cups plain flour
1 teaspoon salt
2 tablespoons oil
Divide dough in half, roll out large enough to cover 2 greased 28cm pizza pans. Heat butter and oil in pan, add onions and peppers, cook, stirring, until onions are lightly browned. Stir in garlic and oregano. Sprinkle half the combined cheeses over the bases; top with onion mixture, then remaining cheeses. Bake in moderately hot oven for 20 minutes or until golden brown.

Clockwise, from top centre: Puff Pizza with Three-Cheese Topping; Quick and Easy Ham and Pineapple Pizza; Onion and Pepper Pizza with Thick Wholemeal Crust; Crispy Crust Pizza with The Lot; Spinach and Feta Cheese Pizza with Wholemeal Crispy Crust; Pantry Seafood Pizza with Soft Crust.

Thick Wholemeal Crust: Combine sugar and yeast with water in bowl, cover, stand in warm place for about 10 minutes or until mixture is foamy. Sift flours and salt into large bowl, stir in yeast mixture, then oil. Knead dough on lightly floured surface for about 10 minutes or until dough is smooth and elastic. Place dough in lightly oiled bowl, cover, stand in warm place for about 45 minutes or until dough has doubled in bulk. Knead dough again until smooth.

CRISPY CRUST PIZZA WITH THE LOT
½ cup canned tomato puree
⅓ cup tomato paste
2 teaspoons dried basil leaves
3 cups (300g) grated tasty cheese
2 onions, chopped
2 green peppers, chopped
2 sticks cabanossi, thinly sliced
⅓ cup sliced black olives
250g baby mushrooms, sliced
½ cup grated parmesan cheese
PIZZA CRUST
7g sachet dried yeast
1 teaspoon sugar
¾ cup hot water
2 cups plain flour
½ teaspoon salt

Divide dough in half, roll out large enough to fit 2 greased 28cm pizza pans. Spread each with combined tomato puree, tomato paste and basil. Top with tasty cheese, onions, peppers, cabanossi, olives and mushrooms. Sprinkle with parmesan cheese, bake in moderately hot oven for 20 minutes or until golden brown.
Pizza Crust: Combine yeast and sugar, stir in water, add to sifted flour and salt in bowl; mix to a firm dough. Turn onto lightly floured surface, knead for about 10 minutes or until quite smooth and elastic.

Picked Pockets

CHILLI CON CARNE-FILLED POCKETS

Filling can be made the day before, covered and refrigerated. Reheat gently when required.

375g minced beef
6 pocket breads
15g butter
1 onion, finely chopped
1 stick celery, chopped
400g can tomatoes
¼ cup tomato sauce
1 tablespoon Worcestershire sauce
1 tablespoon sweet chilli sauce
432g can red kidney beans, drained

Cut breads in half crossways. Melt butter in pan, add onion and celery, cook, stirring, until onion is soft. Add mince, cook, stirring, until well browned. Add undrained crushed tomatoes and sauces, bring to the boil, reduce heat, simmer uncovered 20 minutes; add rinsed beans, reheat. Toast breads on oven tray for about 10 minutes, serve filled with hot mince mixture.

Makes 12.

TACOS WITH RATATOUILLE FILLING

12 taco shells
1 eggplant, peeled, chopped
salt
1 tablespoon oil
1 clove garlic, crushed
1 onion, chopped
2 x 400g cans tomatoes
285g can champignons, drained
2 tablespoons oil, extra
2 teaspoons dried oregano leaves
1 teaspoon sugar
2 canned jalapeno chillies, chopped
4 zucchini, peeled, chopped
200g carton sour cream
1 cup grated tasty cheese

Sprinkle eggplant with salt, stand 30 minutes, rinse under cold water, drain.

Heat oil in pan, add garlic and onion, cook, stirring, until onion is soft. Add undrained crushed tomatoes, bring to the boil, reduce heat, simmer uncovered for about 20 minutes or until the mixture is thick.

Cut champignons in half. Heat extra oil in pan, add oregano, sugar and chillies, cook, stirring, 1 minute, add eggplant, cook, stirring, until eggplant is lightly browned, add zucchini, cook few minutes, stir in champignons and tomato mixture; reheat. Serve in taco shells with sour cream and cheese.

Makes 12.

TACOS WITH SALMON AND AVOCADO

12 taco shells
440g can red salmon, drained
185g can pimientos, drained
1 onion, sliced
1 tablespoon capers, drained
¼ cup French dressing
2 tablespoons lemon juice
1 avocado, chopped
1 small lettuce, shredded

Flake salmon, slice pimientos finely. Combine capers, dressing and lemon juice in bowl, stir in salmon, avocado, pimientos and onion. Fill taco shells with lettuce, top with salmon mixture.

Makes 12.

CRUNCHY TURKEY AND ALMOND-FILLED POCKETS

6 pocket breads
375g smoked turkey breast
½ cup toasted slivered almonds
3 green shallots, finely chopped
½ cup sour cream
2 tablespoons cranberry sauce
¼ cup orange juice
1 small lettuce, shredded
2 carrots, grated

Cut turkey into thin strips. Combine turkey, almonds and shallots in bowl. Combine sour cream, cranberry sauce and orange juice, stir into turkey mixture. Cut pocket breads in half crossways. Place lettuce and carrots into pockets, top with turkey mixture.

Makes 12.

Veal Alternatives

TASTY CRUMBED VEAL WITH THREE SAUCES

Crumbed Veal can be wrapped and frozen for up to three months; thaw before cooking. Serve topped with one of the delicious Sauces below.

4 veal steaks
plain flour
1 egg, lightly beaten
2 tablespoons milk
1 cup dry breadcrumbs
60g butter
2 tablespoons oil

Pound veal with mallet until thin, dust evenly but lightly with flour, dip in combined egg and milk, then breadcrumbs.

Heat butter and oil in large pan, add veal, cook over medium heat until browned on both sides and tender; drain on absorbent paper.

Serves 4.

GREEN PEPPERCORN SAUCE

Sauce is best made just before serving

2 tablespoons canned, drained green peppercorns
15g butter
4 green shallots, chopped
½ cup cream
⅓ cup sour cream
1 tablespoon lemon juice

Rinse peppercorns; drain, crush lightly. Melt butter in pan, add peppercorns and shallots; cook 1 minute, stirring. Stir in cream, sour cream and lemon juice, reheat without boiling.

LEMON CAPER SAUCE

Sauce can be made one day ahead.

15g butter
1 onion, sliced
2 teaspoons cornflour
1 cup chicken stock
2 teaspoons sugar
1 tablespoon lemon juice
1 tablespoon capers, drained

Melt butter in pan, add onion, cook, stirring, 2 minutes or until onion is soft. Blend cornflour with a little of the chicken stock. Stir into pan with remaining stock, sugar and lemon juice. Stir constantly over heat until Sauce boils and thickens; add capers.

MUSHROOM AND TOMATO SAUCE

Sauce can be made one day ahead.

15g butter
1 tablespoon oil
1 onion, chopped
250g baby mushrooms, sliced
1 clove garlic, crushed
1 tablespoon tomato paste
400g can tomatoes
¼ cup dry white wine
½ cup chicken stock

Heat butter and oil in pan, add onion, cook, stirring occasionally, until lightly browned. Add mushrooms and garlic, cook, stirring, until mushrooms are soft. Add tomato paste, undrained crushed tomatoes, wine and stock, bring to the boil, reduce heat, simmer uncovered 20 minutes or until thick.

LEFT: From left: Veal with Green Peppercorn Sauce; Veal with Mushroom and Tomato Sauce; Veal with Lemon Caper Sauce.
BELOW: Back, from left: Chilli Con Carne-Filled Pockets; Tacos with Ratatouille Filling; front, from left: Tacos with Salmon and Avocado; Crunchy Turkey and Almond-Filled Pockets.

Quiches

Quiches are favorites for all occasions and should be regarded as much more than mere snack food. They can be very satisfying as main courses, especially for guests who may be vegetarians.

SPINACH, BACON AND FETA CHEESE QUICHE

PASTRY
1 cup plain flour
90g butter
1 egg yolk
1 tablespoon lemon juice, approximately
FILLING
1 bunch English spinach
2 tablespoons oil
4 bacon rashers, chopped
1 onion, sliced
125g feta cheese
3 eggs
200g carton sour cream
2 tablespoons grated parmesan cheese

Pastry: Sift flour into bowl, rub in butter, add egg yolk and enough lemon juice to mix to a firm dough. Cover, refrigerate 30 minutes. Roll dough out large enough to line a 23cm flan tin, trim edges. Cover Pastry with greaseproof paper, fill with dried beans or rice. Bake in moderately hot oven 7 minutes, remove paper and beans, bake further 7 minutes.

Spread spinach mixture evenly over Pastry, top with feta cheese and bacon mixture. Pour in egg mixture, sprinkle with parmesan cheese. Bake in moderate oven for 30 minutes or until set.
Filling: Chop spinach leaves finely. Heat oil in pan, add spinach, cook, stirring, until spinach is just wilted; drain well. Add bacon and onion to pan, cook, stirring, until onion is soft; drain. Crumble feta cheese; whisk eggs and cream together in bowl.

QUICK ASPARAGUS QUICHE

We used an ovenproof quiche dish: the metal variety with the removable base is unsuitable for this recipe.

15g butter
1 onion, finely chopped
1 clove garlic, crushed
1 cup stale wholemeal breadcrumbs
4 eggs
300g carton sour cream
1 cup grated tasty cheese
¼ cup grated parmesan cheese
1 tablespoon self-raising flour
⅓ cup milk
2 x 340g cans asparagus spears, drained
paprika

Heat butter in pan, add onion, cook, stirring, until onion is soft. Stir in garlic and breadcrumbs. Press evenly over base of 25cm quiche dish. Blend or process combined eggs, sour cream, cheeses, flour and milk until smooth, pour slowly into quiche dish. Top with asparagus, sprinkle lightly with paprika. Bake in moderate oven 35 minutes or until set.

OPPOSITE PAGE: Back: Wholemeal Pumpkin Quiche; front: Salmon and Cheese Quiche.
RIGHT: Back: Quick Asparagus Quiche; front: Spinach, Bacon and Feta Cheese Quiche.

WHOLEMEAL PUMPKIN QUICHE

Boil or steam about 375g pumpkin to give one cup mashed pumpkin. Leftover pumpkin can be used if it has not been mashed with milk, butter, cream.

WHOLEMEAL PASTRY
1 cup wholemeal plain flour
¼ cup wholemeal self-raising flour
¼ cup wheatgerm or unprocessed bran
125g butter
2 tablespoons water, approximately
FILLING
15g butter
1 small onion, finely chopped
3 bacon rashers, chopped
1 cup mashed pumpkin
3 eggs
300ml carton cream
½ cup grated tasty cheese
1 tablespoon chopped chives

Wholemeal Pastry: Sift flours into bowl, add wheatgerm. Rub in butter, add enough water to mix to a firm dough, cover, refrigerate 30 minutes. Roll Pastry out large enough to line a 23cm flan tin, trim edges, line with greaseproof paper, fill with dry beans or rice. Bake in moderately hot oven 7 minutes, remove paper and beans, bake further 7 minutes.

Pour Filling into Pastry case, bake in moderate oven for about 30 minutes or until set.

Filling: Melt butter in pan, add onion and bacon, cook, stirring, until onion is soft; combine pumpkin, eggs, cream, cheese and chives in bowl, whisk in onion mixture.

SALMON AND CHEESE QUICHE
PASTRY
1 cup plain flour
90g butter
1 tablespoon tomato paste
2 tablespoons water, approximately
FILLING
220g can salmon, drained
½ cup grated tasty cheese
4 green shallots, chopped
¾ cup milk
¾ cup cream
3 eggs

Pastry: Sift flour into bowl, rub in butter, add tomato paste and enough water to mix to a firm dough, cover, refrigerate 30 minutes. Roll dough out large enough to line a 23cm flan tin. Cover Pastry with greaseproof paper, cover paper thickly with dried beans or rice. Bake in moderately hot oven 7 minutes, remove paper and beans, bake further 7 minutes, cool. Spread salmon mixture into Pastry case, pour in egg mixture. Bake in moderate oven 30 minutes or until set.

Filling: Flake salmon in bowl with fork, mix in cheese and shallots. Beat milk, cream and eggs together in bowl.

CAMEMBERT AND SMOKED SALMON QUICHE

Smoked salmon off-cuts can be bought cheaply from delicatessens.

6 sheets fillo pastry
45g butter, melted
200g packet camembert cheese
6 eggs
125g smoked salmon
2 x 300ml cartons cream
1 tablespoon chopped fresh dill

Line a greased 25cm quiche dish or flan tin with one sheet of the pastry, brush with butter, top with another sheet of pastry placed the opposite way to the first sheet, brush with butter. Continue layering and buttering pastry in this way. Trim edges of pastry with scissors. Remove rind from camembert, slice camembert thinly, place evenly into pastry case. Blend or process combined eggs, salmon, cream and dill until smooth, pour into pastry case. Bake in moderate oven for about 40 minutes or until set.

SMOKED FISH QUICHE
PASTRY
¾ cup plain flour
½ cup self-raising flour
1 teaspoon dry mustard
90g butter
¼ cup sour cream
2 tablespoons lemon juice, approximately
FILLING
375g smoked fish
1 small red pepper, finely chopped
2 green shallots, finely chopped
½ cup grated tasty cheese
3 eggs
¾ cup sour cream
½ cup milk

Pastry: Sift flours and mustard into bowl, rub in butter. Add sour cream, then enough lemon juice to mix to a firm dough. Roll out large enough to line a 23cm flan tin, trim edges, cover Pastry with greaseproof paper, fill with dry beans or rice. Bake in moderately hot oven 7 minutes, remove paper and beans, bake further 7 minutes. Spread fish mixture into Pastry case, top with egg mixture. Bake in moderate oven for about 30 minutes or until set.

Filling: Poach or microwave fish until tender; drain, flake, remove skin and bones; combine with pepper, shallots and cheese in bowl. Whisk eggs, cream and milk together in bowl.

LEEK AND MUSHROOM QUICHE
CREAM CHEESE PASTRY
125g packet cream cheese
125g butter
1 cup plain flour
2 teaspoons dried basil leaves
FILLING
60g butter
1 tablespoon oil
1 clove garlic, crushed
3 small leeks, finely sliced
250g baby mushrooms, finely sliced
3 eggs
200g carton sour cream
½ cup grated tasty cheese

Cream Cheese Pastry: Have cream cheese and butter at room temperature. Beat cream cheese and butter together until light and fluffy. Stir in sifted flour and basil, turn onto lightly floured surface, knead lightly and quickly until smooth (dough will be soft), cover, refrigerate 1 hour.

Using fingers, push Pastry evenly over base and side of a 23cm flan tin, trim edges.

Cover Pastry with greaseproof paper, fill with dry beans or rice. Bake in moderately hot oven 7 minutes, remove paper and beans, bake further 7 minutes. Spread leek mixture over Pastry case, top with cheese, pour in egg mixture. Bake in moderate oven for about 30 minutes or until set.

Filling: Heat butter, oil and garlic in pan, add leeks, cook, stirring, until soft, add mushrooms, cook, stirring, until soft. Whisk eggs and sour cream together in bowl.

HAM AND CORN QUICHE
PASTRY
1¼ cups plain flour
90g butter
1 egg yolk
1 tablespoon water, approximately
FILLING
100g ham, chopped
130g can corn kernels, drained
1 onion, finely sliced
¾ cup grated tasty cheese
¾ cup sour cream
½ cup milk
3 eggs

Pastry: Sift flour into bowl, rub in butter. Add egg yolk and enough water to mix to a firm dough, cover, refrigerate 30 minutes. Roll dough out large enough to line a 23cm flan tin. Cover Pastry with greaseproof paper, fill with dry beans or rice. Bake in moderately hot oven 7 minutes, remove beans and paper, bake further 7 minutes.

Spread ham mixture over Pastry, pour over egg mixture. Bake in moderate oven for about 30 minutes or until golden brown and set.

Filling: Combine ham, corn, onion and cheese together in bowl. Whisk sour cream, milk and eggs together in bowl.

Back: Smoked Fish Quiche; centre: Leek and Mushroom Quiche; front, from left: Camembert and Smoked Salmon Quiche, Ham and Corn Quiche.

Quick Ways with Barbecued Chicken

Clockwise, from Top: Tomato Mushroom Sauce; Sweet 'n' Spicy Mango Sauce; Spicy Peanut Sauce; Creamy Mushroom Sauce; Curried Chicken Croquettes; Pineapple and Mandarin Sauce; Mild Curried Coconut Sauce.

For short-cut chicken main courses, here are some suggestions using take-away barbecued chickens. The interesting sauces will make all the difference!

SWEET 'N' SPICY MANGO SAUCE
425g can mangoes
2 tablespoons fruit chutney
1 tablespoon white vinegar
1 teaspoon light soy sauce
¼ teaspoon chilli powder

Drain mangoes, reserve ¼ cup syrup. Blend or process combined mangoes, reserved syrup, chutney, vinegar, soy sauce and chilli powder until smooth. Pour into pan, stir over heat until heated through.

Makes about 1 cup.

CURRIED CHICKEN CROQUETTES

Use a size 15 barbecued seasoned chicken to give two and a half cups chopped chicken. The seasoning gives added flavor to the croquettes. Croquettes can be prepared, cooked and refrigerated up to 12 hours before required. Reheat on oven tray uncovered in a moderate oven for about 20 minutes before serving.

2½ cups chopped cooked chicken
60g butter
1 onion, finely chopped
3 bacon rashers, chopped
2 teaspoons curry powder
⅓ cup plain flour
1 cup milk
½ cup seasoning
1 cup grated tasty cheese
2 eggs, lightly beaten
½ cup milk
2 cups dry breadcrumbs
oil for deep frying

Melt butter in pan, add onion, bacon and curry powder, cook, stirring, few minutes; stir in flour, cook further minute. Gradually stir in milk, stir constantly over heat until mixture boils and thickens, remove from heat, stir in chicken, seasoning and cheese. Spread mixture onto tray covered with plastic wrap, refrigerate until cold. Shape mixture into 15 croquettes. Dip croquettes into combined eggs and milk, toss in breadcrumbs. Deep fry croquettes in hot oil a few at a time until golden brown; drain.

Makes about 15.

TOMATO MUSHROOM SAUCE

1 tablespoon oil
1 onion, chopped
1 clove garlic, crushed
1 red pepper, chopped
1 teaspoon dried marjoram leaves
¼ teaspoon chilli powder
1 tablespoon brown sugar
¼ cup red wine
400g can tomatoes
125g baby mushrooms, sliced

Heat oil, add onion and garlic, cook, stirring, until onion is soft. Add pepper, marjoram, chilli, sugar, wine and undrained crushed tomatoes. Bring to the boil, reduce heat, simmer until Sauce is thick. Add mushrooms, simmer further 5 minutes.

Makes about 1½ cups.

CREAMY MUSHROOM SAUCE

30g butter
2 tablespoons oil
1 onion, finely chopped
1 clove garlic, crushed
2 tablespoons seeded mustard
500g baby mushrooms, sliced
½ cup dry white wine
1 tablespoon cornflour
1 cup chicken stock
250g carton light sour cream

Heat butter and oil in pan, add onion, cook, stirring, until soft; add garlic, mustard and mushrooms, cook, stirring, 10 minutes, add wine, cook few minutes. Stir in blended cornflour and stock, stir over heat until Sauce boils and thickens, stir in cream; reheat.

Makes about 2 cups.

SPICY PEANUT SAUCE

30g butter
1 teaspoon curry powder
1 clove garlic, crushed
1 teaspoon grated fresh ginger
¼ cup chopped unsalted roasted peanuts
½ cup peanut butter
¼ cup dry sherry
¾ cup water
1 teaspoon honey
¼ teaspoon tabasco sauce

Melt butter in pan, add curry powder, garlic, ginger and peanuts, stir over heat 2 minutes. Stir in peanut butter, sherry, water, honey and tabasco, stir over heat until thick and smooth.

Makes about 1½ cups.

PINEAPPLE AND MANDARIN SAUCE

440g can pineapple pieces
310g can mandarin segments, drained
1 tablespoon oil
1 clove garlic, crushed
2 green shallots, chopped
¼ cup dry sherry
¼ cup dry white wine
2 teaspoons light soy sauce
2 teaspoons cornflour
1 cup water

Drain pineapple, reserve ½ cup syrup. Heat oil in pan with garlic and shallots, add sherry, wine and soy sauce, then blended cornflour and water. Stir constantly over heat until mixture boils and thickens; add mandarin and pineapple pieces; heat through gently.

Makes about 2 cups.

MILD CURRIED COCONUT SAUCE

30g butter
1 tablespoon oil
1 clove garlic, crushed
1 onion, finely chopped
1 teaspoon curry powder
1 teaspoon paprika
½ teaspoon sugar
1 cup chicken stock
¼ cup dry white wine
1 tablespoon plain flour
200ml carton coconut cream

Heat butter and oil in pan, add garlic and onion, cook, stirring, until onion is soft. Add curry powder, paprika and sugar, cook, stirring, few minutes. Stir in stock and wine, bring to the boil, reduce heat, simmer uncovered 5 minutes. Stir in blended flour and coconut cream, stir constantly until mixture boils and thickens.

Makes about 2 cups.

CHICKEN THIGHS STUFFED WITH SPINACH AND BRIE

Prepare for cooking a day ahead.

6 chicken thighs
250g packet brie cheese
4 bacon rashers, finely chopped
30g butter
1 clove garlic, crushed
1 bunch English spinach
¼ cup oil
fresh rosemary sprigs

Remove excess fat from chicken. Have brie at room temperature, slice brie thinly. Cook bacon in pan until crisp; drain. Add butter to pan with garlic, cook, stirring, 1 minute, add spinach leaves, stir until spinach is just wilted; drain well. Chop spinach finely, combine with bacon.

Carefully ease skin away from flesh of chicken with fingers to make a pocket. Place brie into pocket, top with spinach mixture, pull skin over filling, secure with toothpicks. Place thighs on rack over baking dish, brush with oil, sprinkle with rosemary sprigs, bake uncovered in moderate oven for about 40 minutes or until chicken is golden brown and tender. Baste several times during cooking.

Serves 4 to 6.

CHICKEN DRUMSTICKS WITH BASIL AND CHEESE SEASONING

Prepare for cooking one day ahead.

16 chicken drumsticks
30g butter, melted
BASIL AND CHEESE SEASONING
30g butter
6 green shallots, chopped
1 clove garlic, crushed
¼ cup chopped fresh basil
125g ricotta cheese
¼ cup grated parmesan cheese
¼ cup dry breadcrumbs
1 egg yolk

Loosen skin around drumsticks, push about a tablespoon of Seasoning under the skin into pockets, pull skin over Seasoning. Place drumsticks in single layer in greased baking dish, brush with butter, bake in moderate oven for about 45 minutes or until chicken is tender and well-browned.

Basil and Cheese Seasoning: Heat butter in pan, add shallots and garlic, cook 1 minute, stirring, remove from heat, stir in basil, cheeses, breadcrumbs and egg yolk, mix well.

Serves 8.

LEFT: From top: Chicken Thighs Stuffed with Spinach and Brie; Chicken Marylands with Tarragon Mustard Sauce; Chicken Drumsticks with Basil and Cheese Seasoning.
RIGHT: Back, from left: Pecan-Crumbed Chicken with Mustard Cream; Moist Chicken in Creme Fraiche Marinade; front: Pan-Fried Chicken Fillets with Cumberland Sauce.

CHICKEN MARYLANDS WITH TARRAGON MUSTARD SAUCE

Sauce must be made just before serving; it is unsuitable for reheating.

4 chicken marylands
TARRAGON MUSTARD SAUCE
¼ cup tarragon vinegar
2 tablespoons dry white wine
250g butter
1 tablespoon French mustard
1 tablespoon chopped parsley

Place chicken into greased baking dish in single layer, bake uncovered in moderate oven 45 minutes or until golden brown and tender; drain. Serve hot with Sauce.

Tarragon Mustard Sauce: Heat vinegar and wine in pan until boiling, reduce heat, simmer about 5 minutes or until reduced to about 2 tablespoons. Whisk in cold butter off the heat, about 30g at a time, stirring constantly until slightly thickened, stir in mustard and parsley; serve immediately.

Serves 4.

MOIST CHICKEN IN CREME FRAICHE MARINADE

Creme Fraiche can be made and stored in refrigerator for up to 10 days.

6 chicken breast fillets
CREME FRAICHE
300ml carton thickened cream
300g carton sour cream
ground black pepper

Combine chicken in bowl with Creme Fraiche, cover, refrigerate overnight. Grill chicken very slowly, for about 20 minutes. Brush with Creme Fraiche during the cooking; turn chicken only once during cooking.

Creme Fraiche: Combine cream, sour cream and pepper in bowl, cover, stand at room temperature for 1 to 2 days or until mixture is thick; then cover and refrigerate.

Serves 4 to 6.

PECAN-CRUMBED CHICKEN WITH MUSTARD CREAM

Chicken can be crumbed up to 12 hours before required; store covered and refrigerated.

6 chicken breast fillets
plain flour
2½ cups (250g) pecan nuts
2 eggs
3 tablespoons French mustard
30g butter
¼ cup oil
⅔ cup sour cream

Dust chicken lightly with flour. Blend or process pecans until finely ground. Whisk eggs in bowl with 2 tablespoons of the mustard. Dip chicken into egg mixture, then into pecans. Heat butter and oil in large pan, add chicken, cook until browned on both sides and tender. Remove chicken from pan, keep warm. Add remaining mustard and sour cream to clean pan, stir over low heat without boiling until smooth and heated through; serve with chicken.

Serves 4 to 6.

PAN-FRIED CHICKEN FILLETS WITH CUMBERLAND SAUCE

Sauce can be made one day ahead.

8 chicken breast fillets
30g butter
2 tablespoons oil
CUMBERLAND SAUCE
1 cup red currant jelly
3 teaspoons grated orange rind
3 teaspoons grated lemon rind
1 cup orange juice
½ cup lemon juice
1 teaspoon grated fresh ginger
2 tablespoons port
2 teaspoons French mustard
1 tablespoon cornflour
2 tablespoons water

Heat butter and oil in large pan, add chicken, cook gently over low heat 10 minutes on both sides or until chicken is tender. Serve with Sauce.

Cumberland Sauce: Combine jelly, rinds and juices, ginger, port and mustard in pan, bring to the boil, stir in blended cornflour and water, cook, stirring, until Sauce boils and thickens, reduce heat, simmer 5 minutes.

Serves 8.

Medley of Meats

LOIN OF LAMB WITH MINTY APRICOT SEASONING

Prepare lamb up to six hours ahead of cooking if preferred.

1kg loin of lamb
¼ cup mint jelly
2 tablespoons lemon juice
2 tablespoons brown sugar
MINTY APRICOT SEASONING
½ cup cracked wheat (burghul)
30g butter
1 tablespoon oil
3 small zucchini, grated
1 clove garlic, crushed
1 tablespoon mint jelly
2 tablespoons chopped mint
½ cup chopped dried apricots
1½ cups stale breadcrumbs
1 egg, lightly beaten

Ask butcher to bone loin of lamb leaving a long flap. Open lamb out flat, place Seasoning along centre of lamb, roll up, secure with string at 2cm intervals. Place loin on rack over baking dish, bake in moderate oven for about 45 minutes or until done as desired. Baste lamb during the last 20 minutes with combined mint jelly, lemon juice and brown sugar to give lamb a rich glaze. Serve sliced, hot or cold.

Minty Apricot Seasoning: Cover wheat with boiling water, stand 15 minutes. Drain off water, rinse well under cold water. Dry well on absorbent paper. Heat butter and oil in pan, add zucchini and garlic, cook, stirring, until zucchini is soft. Stir in mint jelly and mint, then wheat, apricots, breadcrumbs and egg, mix well.

Serves 4 to 6.

RACKS OF LAMB WITH HONEY CITRUS GLAZE

Prepare lamb for cooking one day ahead if preferred.

4 racks lamb (4 cutlets on each)
1 teaspoon grated orange rind
1 tablespoon orange juice
1 tablespoon lemon juice
¼ cup honey
1 tablespoon dry sherry
2 teaspoons light soy sauce
1 clove garlic, crushed
2 tablespoons plain flour
1½ cups water

Cover bones of cutlets with foil. Place on rack over baking dish, bake in moderately hot oven 20 minutes, brush with half the combined orange rind, orange and lemon juice, honey, sherry, soy sauce and garlic, bake further 5 minutes, brush with remaining citrus mixture, bake further 5 minutes or until lamb is done as desired. Drain fat from baking dish, leaving about 1 tablespoon of juices. Add flour to pan, stir over heat 1 minute, gradually stir in water, stir until sauce boils and thickens, strain before serving.

Serves 4.

LAMB CHOPS VALENTINE

Valentine chops are boned, split almost in half and opened out.

12 valentine lamb chops
¼ cup red currant jelly
¼ cup white wine vinegar
¼ cup fresh rosemary sprigs
2 tablespoons chopped mint

Place chops in dishes in single layer. Top with combined heated jelly, vinegar, rosemary and mint. Marinate several hours or refrigerate overnight. Grill or pan-fry chops, basting with red currant mixture during cooking.

Serves 6 to 8.

BEEF FILLET WITH TARRAGON WINE SAUCE

1kg beef eye fillet (in 1 piece)
30g butter
2 cups dry white wine
30g butter, extra
4 green shallots, chopped
1 tablespoon plain flour
1 teaspoon dried tarragon leaves
½ cup water
1 tablespoon cream

Heat butter in pan, add beef, cook over high heat until browned all over, remove from pan; transfer beef to ovenproof dish, bake in moderate oven 25 minutes or until beef is done as desired. Stand 5 minutes before slicing. Add wine to pan juices, simmer until liquid is reduced to 1 cup, pour into jug. Melt extra butter in pan, add shallots, stir in flour and tarragon, blend in reserved pan juices, water and cream, stir over heat until Sauce boils and thickens; serve over sliced beef.

Serves 4.

PORK WITH APRICOT GLAZE

500g pork fillets
60g butter
1 onion, sliced
2 teaspoons curry powder
2 teaspoons grated fresh ginger
2 tablespoons apricot jam
2 tablespoons light soy sauce
1 tablespoon lemon juice

Melt butter in pan, add onion, curry powder, ginger, jam, soy sauce and lemon juice, stir over low heat until jam is melted. Place pork in greased shallow ovenproof dish in single layer, pour sauce over, bake uncovered in moderate oven for about 25 minutes or until pork is tender (or microwave on HIGH for about 8 minutes).

Serves 4.

LEFT: From left: Pork with Apricot Glaze; Beef Fillet with Tarragon Wine Sauce; Garlic Pepper Pork.

GARLIC PEPPER PORK

500g pork fillets
1 tablespoon ground black pepper
4 cloves garlic, crushed
2 tablespoons oil
1 tablespoon plain flour
1 cup chicken stock

Place pork in small ovenproof dish, press combined pepper and garlic onto exposed surface. Add oil to dish, bake in moderately hot oven 15 minutes or until pork is tender. Remove from dish, slice thickly, keep warm.

Drain all but 1 tablespoon of oil from the dish, stir in flour, stir over heat until lightly browned. Stir in stock, keep stirring over heat until sauce boils and thickens; serve over pork.

Serves 4.

BELOW: Back, from left: Loin of Lamb with Minty Apricot Seasoning; Lamb Chops Valentine; front: Racks of Lamb with Honey Citrus Glaze.

VEGETABLE PARCELS

Vegetables of all types can be presented in excitingly different ways by turning them into surprise packages. Imaginative fillings can vary from rich, nutty and savory to smoothly creamy or satisfyingly hot and spicy.

STUFFED POTATOES

All of the five fillings for the Stuffed Potatoes are enough for six medium-sized potatoes.

Use old, even-sized potatoes; scrub and dry potatoes, prick all over with a skewer. Place potatoes slightly apart directly onto oven rack in moderate oven, bake for about 1 hour or until potatoes are tender (or microwave on HIGH for about 10 minutes). Remove from oven, cut potatoes in half, scoop out the flesh leaving a 1cm thick shell of potato. Brush potatoes, inside and out, lightly with oil, place onto oven tray, cut side up; bake in hot oven 10 minutes. Potatoes are now ready for preferred filling.

Individual recipes will indicate if the scooped-out potato flesh is to be used as part of the filling or not.

SOUR CREAM AND MUSHROOM

Potato flesh is used in this recipe.

15g butter
1 onion, finely chopped
2 bacon rashers, finely chopped
1 clove garlic, crushed
500g small mushrooms, sliced
300g carton sour cream
½ cup grated tasty cheese

Heat butter in pan, add onion and bacon, cook, stirring, for about 5 minutes or until onion is soft, add garlic and mushrooms, cook over low heat 5 minutes or until mushrooms are soft; stir in sour cream and mashed potato. Spoon filling into potatoes on oven tray, sprinkle with cheese; bake in moderate oven 15 minutes or until golden brown.

ALMOND AND VEGETABLE

Potato flesh is used in this recipe.

375g broccoli
2 carrots, thinly sliced
30g butter, melted
1 tablespoon lemon juice
½ cup grated tasty cheese
½ cup flaked almonds
paprika

Cut broccoli into flowerets. Boil, steam or microwave broccoli and carrots until tender. Fill potato halves with chopped potato flesh, broccoli and carrots, brush with combined butter and lemon juice . Top with combined cheese and almonds, sprinkle with paprika; bake in moderate oven on oven tray for 15 minutes or until golden brown.

BEAN 'N' CHILLI

Potato flesh is not used in this recipe.

2 tablespoons oil
30g butter
1 onion, chopped
2 small canned jalapeno chillies,
   chopped
185g can pimientos, drained, sliced
425g can pinto beans, drained
¼ cup sour cream
½ cup grated tasty cheese
1 cup grated tasty cheese, extra

Heat oil and butter in pan, add onion, cook, stirring, few minutes or until onion is soft. Add chillies and pimientos, cook 1 minute. Mash half the beans, stir into onion mixture with sour cream and cheese, stir in remaining beans. Spoon filling into potato halves on oven tray, top with extra cheese; bake in moderate oven for about 15 minutes or until golden brown.

SMOKED FISH AND SHALLOT

Potato flesh is used in this recipe. We used smoked cod in the filling.

500g smoked fish
30g butter
6 green shallots, chopped
1 tablespoon plain flour
1 cup milk
2 tablespoons mayonnaise
2 teaspoons chopped capers
1 teaspoon dried tarragon leaves

Poach fish in simmering water for about 5 minutes or until just tender (or microwave, covered with 1 cup water, on HIGH for about 4 minutes); drain. Remove skin and bones from fish, flake fish with fork. Heat butter in pan, add shallots and flour, cook, stirring, 1 minute. Gradually stir in milk; stir constantly over heat until mixture boils and thickens. Stir in mashed potato, fish, mayonnaise, capers and tarragon. Spoon filling into potatoes on oven tray; bake in moderate oven for about 15 minutes or until heated through.

SLOPPY JOE

Potato flesh is not used in this recipe.

500g minced beef
1 tablespoon oil
1 onion, chopped
2 sticks celery, chopped
440g can baked beans in tomato
   sauce
¼ cup barbecue sauce
¼ cup tomato sauce
½ teaspoon dried mixed herbs
2 tablespoons chopped parsley

Heat oil in pan, add onion and celery, cook, stirring over heat until onion is soft. Add mince, stirring until well browned; cover, cook gently for about 10 minutes or until mince is tender; pour off excess oil. Stir in beans and sauces, bring to the boil, reduce heat, simmer covered 5 minutes. Stir in herbs and parsley, spoon filling into potatoes; serve immediately.

From left: Stuffed Potatoes: Almond and Vegetable; Sour Cream and Mushroom, Bean 'n' Chilli; Smoked Fish and Shallot; Sloppy Joe.

MUSHROOMS WITH BRIE TOPPING

Bread circles can be made the day before required and stored in an airtight container. Have mushrooms ready for reheating 12 hours ahead.

8 large flat mushrooms
1 tablespoon oil
8 slices bread
60g butter, melted
30g butter, extra
2 teaspoons oil, extra
2 onions, sliced
2 bacon rashers, chopped
125g packet brie or camembert, sliced

Remove stems from mushrooms, brush both sides of mushrooms lightly with oil. Place mushrooms on oven tray, bake in moderate oven 10 minutes. Cut out circles of bread, brush both sides of bread with butter, place on oven tray, toast in moderate oven 10 minutes or until golden brown. Heat extra butter and extra oil in pan, add onions, cook over low heat for about 10 minutes or until onions are lightly browned. Add bacon, cook, stirring, for about 3 minutes; drain mixture on absorbent paper. Divide onion mixture evenly between mushrooms, top with brie and toasted bread, place on oven tray, bake in moderate oven 10 minutes or until heated through.
    Makes 8.

MUSHROOMS WITH CURRIED CRAB

Mushrooms can be prepared to the stage of cooking, covered and refrigerated, up to two hours beforehand.

8 large flat mushrooms
30g butter
3 green shallots, finely chopped
2 tablespoons plain flour
2 teaspoons curry powder
¾ cup cream
1 tablespoon lemon juice
180g can crab, drained
paprika
TOPPING
30g butter
1 cup stale breadcrumbs
½ cup grated tasty cheese

Remove stems from mushrooms. Heat butter in pan, add shallots, stir in flour and curry powder, stir constantly over heat 1 minute. Gradually add cream, stir constantly over heat until mixture boils and thickens. Remove from heat, stir in lemon juice and flaked crab. Fill mushroom caps with crab mixture, sprinkle with Topping and paprika; place on oven tray, bake in moderately hot oven 10 minutes.

Topping: Melt butter in pan, add breadcrumbs, stir over heat until breadcrumbs are golden brown, remove from heat; mix in cheese.
    Makes 8.

HOT AND SPICY STUFFED GOLDEN NUGGET PUMPKINS

Make the day before if preferred; reheat covered in moderate oven for about 20 minutes.

6 golden nugget pumpkins
¼ cup oil
FILLING
500g lean minced beef
15g butter
2 teaspoons oil
1 onion, chopped
2 bacon rashers
½ teaspoon chilli powder
2 teaspoons ground cumin
1 clove garlic, crushed
2 tablespoons tomato paste
¼ cup dry white wine
400g can tomatoes
432g can red kidney beans, drained

Cut a 3cm lid from each pumpkin, scoop out seeds. Brush inside and out of each pumpkin with oil, place pumpkins on oven tray, place oiled lids on top; bake in moderate oven 30 minutes. Place Filling into pumpkins, top with lid, return to tray, bake in moderate oven 30 minutes or until pumpkins are tender.

Filling: Heat butter and oil in large pan, add onion, bacon, chilli and cumin, stir over heat few minutes or until onion is soft, pour into bowl. Add beef to pan, cook, stirring, until well browned; add onion mixture, garlic, tomato paste, wine, undrained crushed tomatoes and beans. Cook over low heat, stirring occasionally, for about 20 minutes or until mixture is thick.
    Serves 6.

RIGHT: Hot and Spicy Stuffed Golden Nugget Pumpkins.
BELOW: From left: Mushrooms with Brie Topping; Mushrooms with Curried Crab.

RED PEPPERS WITH CHICKEN AND PINE NUTS

If small red peppers are unavailable use three large peppers cut in half crossways. Make the day before if preferred; refrigerate until ready to serve.

1 barbecued chicken
6 small red peppers
¼ cup pine nuts
2 tablespoons sultanas
1 tomato, peeled, chopped
3 green shallots, chopped
⅓ cup mayonnaise

Remove tops from red peppers, remove seeds. Toast pine nuts on oven tray in moderate oven for about 5 minutes. Remove skin and bones from chicken, chop flesh finely. Combine chicken with pine nuts, sultanas, tomato, shallots and mayonnaise in bowl, mix well. Fill peppers with chicken mixture, refrigerate until ready to serve.
Serves 6.

PEPPER RINGS WITH WILD RICE

Brown rice can be substituted for wild rice if preferred.

3 large yellow peppers
2 tablespoons oil
3 bacon rashers, chopped
1 onion, chopped
½ cup wild rice
2 tablespoons chopped fresh basil
1 litre (4 cups) chicken stock
½ cup white rice
440g can corn kernels
190g can champignons, drained, sliced
2 tablespoons chopped fresh basil, extra

Core and seed whole peppers, drop into a pan of boiling water, return to the boil, boil 1 minute; drain immediately, rinse under cold water until cold; drain. Slice peppers thickly.

Heat oil in large pan, add bacon and onion, cook, stirring few minutes or until onion is soft, add wild rice, stir until all grains are coated with oil; add basil and stock. Bring to the boil, cover, reduce heat, simmer 30 minutes, add rice, cover, simmer 15 minutes or until cooked; drain away any excess stock; cool. Combine corn, champignons and extra basil with rice mixture, spoon into pepper rings. Serve hot or cold.
Serves 6.

Back, from left: Red Peppers with Chicken and Pine Nuts; Salmon Salad-Filled Peppers; front: Pepper Rings with Wild Rice.

SALMON SALAD-FILLED PEPPERS

2 green peppers
440g can red salmon, drained
¼ cup mayonnaise
6 green shallots, chopped
2 sticks celery, chopped
2 tablespoons lime juice
2 tablespoons chutney

Cut peppers in half lengthways, remove seeds. Flake salmon, add to combined mayonnaise, shallots, celery, lime juice and chutney, spoon into peppers, refrigerate several hours before serving.

Makes 4.

RISONI-FILLED TOMATOES WITH BASIL SAUCE

Risoni is a rice-shaped pasta available from most supermarkets. Any variety of small pasta can be substituted.

6 tomatoes
½ cup risoni
30g butter
1 onion, finely chopped
1 stick celery, chopped
¼ cup plain flour
1 cup milk
½ cup grated tasty cheese
½ cup stale breadcrumbs
½ cup grated tasty cheese, extra
2 tablespoons grated parmesan
 cheese
BASIL SAUCE
½ cup fresh basil leaves
¼ cup sour cream
¼ cup Italian dressing
1 tablespoon grated parmesan
 cheese

Cut tops from tomatoes, scoop out flesh. Add risoni to large pan of boiling water, boil rapidly, uncovered, for about 8 minutes or until risoni is tender; drain.

Melt butter in pan, add onion and celery, cook, stirring over heat few minutes or until onion is soft. Stir in flour, stir over heat 1 minute, gradually stir in milk; stir constantly over heat until mixture boils and thickens. Remove from heat, stir in cheese and risoni. Fill tomatoes with risoni mixture, top with combined breadcrumbs, extra cheese and parmesan cheese. Bake in moderately hot oven on oven tray for about 10 minutes or until heated through. Serve with Sauce.

Basil Sauce: Blend or process all ingredients until smooth.

Makes 6.

TOMATOES WITH TUNA AND EGG

Make several hours ahead if desired; refrigerate until ready to serve.

6 tomatoes
425g can tuna in brine, drained
4 hard-boiled eggs, chopped
8 pitted black olives, chopped
4 anchovy fillets, chopped
2 teaspoons curry powder
⅓ cup mayonnaise
4 slices bread

Remove a 2cm slice from the base of each tomato, scoop out pulp carefully, reserve ⅓ cup for the filling. Combine reserved tomato pulp in bowl with flaked tuna, eggs, olives, anchovies, curry powder and mayonnaise. Cut bread into small cubes, toast on oven tray in moderate oven for about 10 minutes or until golden brown. Add half the toast cubes to tuna mixture. Fill tomatoes with tuna mixture, sprinkle with remaining toast cubes just before serving.

Makes 6.

TOMATOES WITH BASIL AND CHEESE FILLING

6 tomatoes
2 tablespoons fresh basil leaves
250g ricotta cheese
½ cup cottage cheese
1 clove garlic, crushed
2 tablespoons French dressing
1 tablespoon chopped fresh basil,
 extra

Slice about 2cm from top of each tomato, scoop out pulp carefully with teaspoon. Blend or process tomato pulp with basil until smooth. Combine ricotta and cottage cheese in bowl; mix well, stir in garlic, dressing and extra basil. Spoon cheese mixture into tomatoes; refrigerate several hours before serving; serve topped with tomato pulp mixture.

Makes 6.

EGGPLANT AND LAMB WITH CHEESY TOPPING

375g minced lamb
3 eggplants
salt
1 tablespoon oil
1 onion, chopped
2 cloves garlic, crushed
¼ cup tomato paste
2 tablespoons chopped fresh basil
2 tablespoons oil, extra
CHEESY TOPPING
90g butter
¾ cup plain flour
1 cup milk
200g carton sour cream
200g ricotta cheese, chopped
125g Swiss cheese, grated
30g butter, extra
1 tablespoon oil
1½ cups stale breadcrumbs
1 tablespoon chopped fresh basil

Slice eggplants in half lengthways, carefully scoop out flesh leaving a 2.5cm thick shell, sprinkle inside of eggplants with salt; stand 30 minutes. Rinse eggplants under water to remove salt, drain on absorbent paper. Heat oil in large pan, add onion and garlic, cook, stirring 1 minute; add lamb, cook, stirring until lamb is well browned, stir in tomato paste and basil; cool.

Brush eggplants all over with extra oil, place lamb filling into eggplants, spread with Topping, sprinkle with crumbs. Place eggplants on oven tray, bake in moderate oven 30 minutes.

Cheesy Topping: Heat butter in pan, add flour, cook, stirring 1 minute, gradually stir in milk and sour cream, stir constantly over heat until sauce boils and thickens. Remove from heat, add cheeses, stir until melted; cool. Heat extra butter and oil in pan, add breadcrumbs, cook, stirring, until golden brown; stir in basil.

Makes 6.

ABOVE RIGHT: From top: Onions Stuffed with Sausages and Rice; Stuffed Artichokes with Olives and Anchovies; Eggplant and Lamb with Cheesy Topping.
RIGHT: From left: Risoni-Filled Tomatoes with Basil Sauce; Tomatoes with Tuna and Egg; Tomatoes with Basil and Cheese Filling.

ONIONS STUFFED WITH SAUSAGES AND RICE

Any type of rice can be substituted for wild rice in this recipe; you will need a half cup cooked rice. Peel onions leaving root end intact.

6 onions
½ cup wild rice
60g butter
250g bratwurst sausages
125g baby mushrooms, sliced
1 tablespoon tomato paste

Add wild rice to large pan of rapidly boiling water, boil rapidly, uncovered, for about 30 minutes or until tender; drain. Boil, steam or microwave onions until just tender; drain. Cut onions in half lengthways, remove centre of onions leaving about 3 outside layers intact; chop onion centres finely. Melt half the butter in pan, add sausages, fry until golden brown and cooked through, remove, drain; chop roughly. Melt remaining butter in pan, add chopped onion, cook, stirring, until lightly browned. Add sausages, mushrooms and rice, cook few minutes or until mushrooms are tender; stir in tomato paste. Spoon mixture into onions, place into baking dish, add about 1cm hot water to dish, cover with foil; bake in moderate oven 15 minutes or until onions are hot. (Or cover, microwave on HIGH about 8 minutes.)
Serves 6.

STUFFED ARTICHOKES WITH OLIVES AND ANCHOVIES

6 globe artichokes
30g butter
1 tablespoon oil
2 cloves garlic, crushed
4 cups stale breadcrumbs
½ cup chopped pitted black olives
½ cup chopped pitted green olives
½ cup chopped slivered almonds
45g can anchovy fillets drained, chopped
30g butter, extra
½ cup oil, extra
½ cup dry white wine
¼ cup lemon juice

Cut stems from artichokes so they sit flat. Remove old outside leaves, shorten tips of remaining leaves with scissors. Heat butter, oil and garlic in pan, add 2 cups of the crumbs, cook, stirring until golden brown. Stir in remaining crumbs, olives, almonds, anchovies and extra butter, mix well.
To stuff artichokes: Lightly tap artichokes on flat surface to loosen leaves, separate leaves carefully. Starting from the outside, press stuffing between leaves until artichokes are packed tightly. Place artichokes in baking dish, pour over combined extra oil, wine and lemon juice, bake uncovered in moderate oven for about 30 minutes, basting occasionally with oil mixture.
Serves 6.

SEAFOOD BARBECUE

During the long, lazy days of summer, who wants to spend hours in the kitchen? Seafood, cooked to succulent perfection on the barbecue, accompanied by vegetable and salad dishes and topped off with a luscious dessert, is the finest solution. The recipes given here will serve 10 people.

SMOKED SALMON PATE

Trimmings and offcuts from smoked salmon can be bought quite cheaply from specialist shops.

125g smoked salmon
100g can smoked salmon spread
250g packet cream cheese
¼ cup cream
1 tablespoon lemon flavored mustard
4 green shallots, chopped

Blend or process salmon and spread until smooth, add remaining ingredients; process until smooth. Serve with crackers and fresh vegetables.

Makes about 2 cups.

CHILLI BARBECUED PRAWNS

2kg green king prawns
1 tablespoon dried black peppercorns
1 tablespoon dried green peppercorns
1 cup French dressing
1 cup dry vermouth
½ cup lime juice
½ cup oil
2 cloves garlic, crushed
2 tablespoons chopped fresh dill
1 small fresh red chilli, finely chopped

Carefully cut a slit in underside of prawns leaving shells intact. Blend or crush peppercorns coarsely. Combine prawns with pepper and remaining ingredients, cover, marinate several hours or refrigerate overnight. Barbecue drained prawns in batches on hot plate (or pan-fry) until prawns are tender and changed in color.

BACON-WRAPPED MUSSELS

Prepare mussels up to 12 hours ahead if preferred.

750g mussels
5 bacon rashers
¼ cup olive oil
1 teaspoon grated lemon rind

Scrub and beard mussels. Bring a large pan of water to the boil; add mussels, remove from pan as soon as shells open, discard any unopened shells. Remove mussel meat from shells. Cut bacon in half crossways, then lengthways. Wrap mussels in bacon, secure bacon with toothpicks. Combine oil and lemon rind in bowl with mussels, mix well. Barbecue or grill mussels over high heat on both sides until bacon is crisp; serve immediately.

Makes about 20.

LEMONY FISH FILLETS WITH ANCHOVY BUTTER

We used whiting fillets in this recipe.

10 white fish fillets
2 tablespoons lemon juice
ANCHOVY BUTTER
125g butter
45g can anchovy fillets, drained
1 clove garlic, crushed
½ teaspoon Worcestershire sauce
2 green shallots, finely chopped
½ teaspoon seeded mustard
2 teaspoons lemon juice

Place each fish fillet on piece of foil, brush fish with lemon juice. Spread with Anchovy Butter. Wrap fish in foil. Barbecue or bake until fish is tender.
Anchovy Butter: Blend or process all ingredients until smooth.

RATATOUILLE KEBABS

Prepare one day ahead if preferred.

1 eggplant
2 bunches spring onions
6 zucchini
2 red peppers
250g punnet cherry tomatoes
½ cup olive oil
¼ cup dry white wine
1 clove garlic, crushed
2 tablespoons chopped parsley
½ teaspoon dried mixed herbs
1 small fresh red chilli, finely chopped

Cut eggplant into cubes, sprinkle with salt, stand 30 minutes, rinse under cold water; drain on absorbent paper. Top and tail onions, cut onions in half lengthways. Cut zucchini and peppers into pieces.

Combine oil in large dish with wine, garlic, parsley, herbs and chilli, mix well. Add eggplant to dish with onions, zucchini, peppers and tomatoes, mix well, stand for at least one hour. Thread vegetables onto skewers.

Barbecue or grill kebabs over low heat on both sides until vegetables are just tender; serve immediately.

PREVIOUS PAGE: Top: Leafy Green Walnut and Mushroom Salad; centre, from left to right: Cheese and Salami Loaf; Seafood Cocktail Salads with Pineapple Dressing; Mixed Green Vegetable and Pasta Salad; bottom: Chilli Barbecued Prawns; Lemony Fish Fillets with Anchovy Butter; Smoked Salmon Pate; Ratatouille Kebabs; Bacon-Wrapped Mussels.
LEFT: Back: Smoked Salmon Pate; front: Bacon-Wrapped Mussels.
RIGHT: Top: Lemony Fish Fillets with Anchovy Butter; centre: Ratatouille Kebabs; bottom: Chilli Barbecued Prawns.

LEAFY GREEN WALNUT AND MUSHROOM SALAD

1 cos lettuce
1 mignonette lettuce
1 butter lettuce
1 witlof (Belgian Endive)
125g baby mushrooms, sliced
½ cup walnut halves
½ cup olive oil
2 tablespoons walnut oil
2 tablespoons lemon juice
1 tablespoon red wine vinegar
1 clove garlic, crushed

Combine roughly torn lettuce leaves and witlof in large salad bowl with mushrooms and walnuts. Combine oils in jar with lemon juice, vinegar and garlic, shake well. Pour strained dressing over salad just before serving.

CHEESE AND SALAMI LOAF

Uncooked Loaf can be wrapped and frozen for up to three months; thaw at room temperature before cooking. Loaf can be baked in a moderate oven for about 25 minutes if preferred.

1 Vienna loaf
SALAMI BUTTER
185g butter
100g salami, finely chopped
¼ cup grated parmesan cheese
2 tablespoons chopped fresh basil

Cut Vienna loaf crossways at 1.5cm intervals, cutting nearly all the way through; spread slices with two thirds of the Butter. Cut diagonally across loaf at 1.5cm intervals, cutting nearly all the way through; spread slices with remaining Butter. Wrap loaf in foil, barbecue loaf 15 minutes. Open foil, barbecue further 10 minutes; serve.

Salami Butter: Have butter at room temperature, combine with salami, cheese and basil.

SEAFOOD COCKTAIL SALADS WITH PINEAPPLE DRESSING

1kg cooked prawns
2 x 440g cans pineapple pieces
440g can red salmon, drained
2 red peppers, sliced
1 cup watercress leaves
10 lettuce leaves
½ cup chopped parsley
PINEAPPLE DRESSING
½ cup mayonnaise
2 tablespoons cream
2 tablespoons tomato sauce

Shell and devein prawns, leaving tails intact. Break salmon into large pieces. Drain pineapple, reserve ¼ cup syrup for Dressing. Combine prawns, salmon, pineapple, peppers and watercress in lettuce leaves on serving plate, sprinkle with parsley. Pour Dressing over just before serving.

Pineapple Dressing: Combine reserved syrup with remaining ingredients in bowl; mix well.

MIXED GREEN VEGETABLE AND PASTA SALAD

500g pasta
2 teaspoons oil
2 x 250g bunches asparagus
6 zucchini
250g snow peas
DRESSING
¼ cup lemon juice
¼ cup oil
¼ cup chopped fresh basil
1 teaspoon sugar

Add pasta gradually to large pan of boiling water, boil rapidly uncovered for about 10 minutes or until just tender; drain, rinse under cold water; drain. Place pasta in bowl with oil, mix oil through pasta with hands. Trim asparagus, cut asparagus and zucchini into 4cm lengths, top and tail snow peas. Boil, steam or microwave asparagus until just tender, rinse under cold water; drain. Boil, steam or microwave zucchini and snow peas until just tender; drain, rinse under cold water; drain. Combine pasta and vegetables with Dressing just before serving.

Dressing: Combine all ingredients in jar; shake well.

RIGHT: Back: Leafy Green Walnut and Mushroom Salad; Seafood Cocktail Salads with Pineapple Dressing; front: Cheese and Salami Loaf; Mixed Green Vegetable and Pasta Salad.

SUMMERTIME ROCKMELON FLAN

Top filling with rockmelon balls one hour before serving.

PASTRY
1 cup plain flour
2 tablespoons icing sugar
90g butter
1 egg yolk
1 tablespoon water, approx.
FILLING
1½ kg rockmelon
¼ cup sugar
2 teaspoons grated orange rind
½ cup orange juice
2 teaspoons gelatine
1 tablespoon water
1 cup thickened cream
⅓ cup apricot jam
1 tablespoon Grand Marnier

Pastry: Sift flour and icing sugar into bowl, rub in butter. Add egg yolk and enough water to mix to a firm dough. Roll dough out onto floured surface, large enough to line 23cm flan tin. Cover Pastry with greaseproof paper, cover paper thickly with beans or rice. Bake in moderately hot oven 7 minutes, remove paper and beans, bake further 7 minutes; cool.

Fill Pastry case with rockmelon mixture, refrigerate until set, top with rockmelon balls, brush with jam mixture, refrigerate 1 hour or until set.

Filling: Scoop melon into balls. Scoop out remaining flesh, chop roughly; reserve ½ cup. Blend or process reserved rockmelon with sugar, orange rind and juice. Sprinkle gelatine over water, dissolve over hot water (or microwave on HIGH 40 seconds), cool to room temperature, add to melon mixture; stir in cream. Heat jam in pan, strain, stir in Grand Marnier.

HONEY ROLL

Roll can be completed and stored in an airtight container a day before serving, if preferred. We used ginger preserved in syrup in this recipe.

60g butter
¾ cup golden syrup
¾ cup plain flour
½ cup self-raising flour
2 teaspoons ground ginger
1 teaspoon ground cinnamon
½ teaspoon ground nutmeg
¼ teaspoon ground cloves
2 eggs, lightly beaten
1 teaspoon bicarbonate of soda
¼ cup boiling water
½ cup coconut
GINGER CREAM FILLING
300ml carton thickened cream
2 teaspoons ginger syrup
¼ cup finely chopped preserved ginger

Cream butter and golden syrup until light and fluffy in small bowl with electric mixer; transfer to large bowl. Stir in sifted flours and spices, then eggs and combined soda and water. Pour mixture into greased and lined Swiss roll tin (base measures 25cm x 30cm). Bake in moderate oven for about 15 minutes. Cover wire rack with greaseproof paper, sprinkle with coconut, turn cake onto paper, roll up cake loosely from long side. Stand few minutes, unroll, cool to room temperature. Spread with Filling; re-roll carefully.

Ginger Cream Filling: Beat cream and syrup until peaks form, fold in ginger.

ABOVE: Summertime Rockmelon Flan.
BELOW: Honey Roll.

SWEET AND SAUCY

A simple serving of icecream assumes gourmet proportions when topped with a rich and creamy or refreshingly fruity sauce. Ring the changes with our selection of recipes.

PAWPAW GINGER SAUCE
3 cups chopped pawpaw
½ cup sugar
½ cup water
¼ cup lemon juice
1 teaspoon grated fresh ginger
Combine sugar and water in pan, bring to the boil, reduce heat, add pawpaw, simmer 10 minutes, or until pawpaw is soft, add lemon juice and ginger; cool. Blend or process until smooth; refrigerate before serving.
Makes about 2 cups.

CHOC-MINT LIQUEUR SAUCE
Creme de Cacao is a chocolate-flavored liqueur.

⅔ cup thickened cream
2 tablespoons Creme de Cacao
1 tablespoon Creme de Menthe
1 tablespoon icing sugar
few drops peppermint essence
Combine all ingredients thoroughly.
Makes about 1 cup.

RICH BUTTERSCOTCH SAUCE
1 cup brown sugar, firmly packed
30g butter
1 tablespoon liquid glucose
½ cup evaporated milk
½ cup thickened cream
Combine sugar, butter and glucose in pan, stir constantly over heat without boiling, until sugar is dissolved. Remove from heat, stir in milk and cream. Serve warm or cold.
Makes about 2 cups.

BLUEBERRY BUTTER SAUCE
¼ cup sugar
¾ cup water
3 teaspoons cornflour
1 tablespoon lemon juice
1 cup fresh or frozen blueberries
30g butter
½ teaspoon cinnamon
Combine sugar and water in pan, stir in blended cornflour and lemon juice. Stir constantly over heat until mixture boils and thickens. Add blueberries, simmer few minutes. Add butter and cinnamon, stir over heat until butter is melted. Blend or process until smooth, strain, serve hot or cold.
Makes 1½ cups.

HOT ORANGE SABAYON SAUCE
2 egg yolks
1 teaspoon grated orange rind
¼ cup sugar
¼ cup orange juice
¼ cup dry white wine
Combine egg yolks, orange rind and sugar in top of double boiler over simmering water. Beat mixture with rotary beater or electric mixer until pale in color. Gradually beat in orange juice and wine. Beat constantly until doubled in volume; serve immediately.
Makes about 2 cups.

MOCHA MOUSSE SAUCE
100g dark chocolate, melted
2 teaspoons instant coffee powder
1 tablespoon hot water
1 tablespoon Tia Maria or Kahlua
½ cup thickened cream
Combine chocolate, dissolved coffee and water and Tia Maria in bowl; cool to room temperature. Beat cream until soft peaks form, fold into chocolate mixture, serve immediately.
Makes 1½ cups.

BELOW: Sauces: Clockwise from top left: Pawpaw Ginger; Choc-Mint Liqueur; Rich Butterscotch; Hot Orange Sabayon; Mocha Mousse; right: Blueberry Butter.

A wonderful dessert can transform a dinner party into a really memorable occasion.

FROZEN CHOCOLATE PECAN CAKE
PECAN CRUST
1½ cups (200g) pecan nuts, finely chopped
⅓ cup brown sugar
60g butter, melted
2 teaspoons rum
CHOCOLATE FILLING
100g dark chocolate, melted
2 teaspoons instant coffee powder
2 teaspoons hot water
2 eggs, lightly beaten
2 teaspoons rum
2 teaspoons vanilla
300ml carton thickened cream
Pecan Crust: Toast pecan nuts on oven tray in moderate oven for about 5 minutes, cool. Combine pecan nuts in bowl with brown sugar, butter and rum, mix well; press evenly and firmly over base and side of 23cm flan tin with removable base, freeze 30 minutes. Pour Filling over Crust, freeze several hours or overnight if possible. Decorate with extra whipped cream, strawberries and extra chopped pecan nuts if desired.
Chocolate Filling: Place cooled chocolate in large bowl, add dissolved coffee and water, then stir in eggs, rum and vanilla. Beat cream until soft peaks form, fold into chocolate mixture.

FROZEN ICECREAM CHEESECAKE WITH WARM MARSALA SAUCE
60g butter, melted
1 cup (125g) sweet biscuits, crushed
5 egg yolks
½ cup castor sugar
½ cup marsala
250g packet cream cheese
2 litres vanilla icecream
WARM MARSALA SAUCE
60g butter
1 cup brown sugar, lightly packed
¼ cup marsala
½ cup thickened cream
Combine butter and biscuit crumbs, mix well. Press evenly and firmly over base of 20cm springform pan, refrigerate 30 minutes.

Place egg yolks and sugar into top of double boiler, beat with rotary beater or electric mixer over simmering water until pale in color, add marsala, beat constantly over simmering water until mixture thickens, cool to room temperature. Have cream cheese at room temperature. Beat cream cheese in large bowl with electric mixer until smooth, gradually beat in marsala mixture, fold in slightly softened icecream. Pour into springform pan, cover, freeze overnight. Allow to stand 15 minutes before serving with Sauce.
Warm Marsala Sauce: Combine butter, sugar and marsala in pan, stir over low heat until butter is melted and mixture heated through. Add cream, stir until mixture is smooth.

TWO-CHOCOLATE ICECREAM CAKE
Can be made up to three days ahead.

½ cup blanched almonds, chopped
400g dark chocolate, chopped
400g milk chocolate, chopped
4 eggs
½ cup sugar
2 x 300ml cartons thickened cream
2 tablespoons Grand Marnier
Toast almonds on oven tray in moderate oven for about 5 minutes; cool. Melt dark chocolate and milk chocolate in two separate bowls over hot water, cool; do not allow to set. Beat eggs and sugar in small bowl with electric mixer until thick and creamy. Beat cream in large bowl until firm peaks form, fold in Grand Marnier and almonds, then the egg mixture in 2 batches. Divide mixture evenly into 2 bowls. Stir dark chocolate into 1 bowl of cream mixture and milk chocolate into the other bowl. Line base of 23cm springform pan with foil, place side around base, trim away excess foil. Pour milk chocolate mixture into pan, cover with foil, freeze 1 hour or until set. Top with dark chocolate mixture, cover with foil, freeze overnight. Serve with fruit if desired.

CHOCOLATE ALMOND TORTONI WITH CHERRIES
2 x 300ml cartons thickened cream
4 egg whites
½ cup castor sugar
100g dark chocolate, melted
½ cup slivered almonds
100g dark chocolate, melted, extra
½ cup chopped red glace cherries
½ cup chopped green glace cherries
Beat cream until firm peaks form. Beat egg whites in small bowl with electric mixer until soft peaks form, gradually beat in sugar a tablespoon at a time; beat until dissolved; transfer to large bowl, fold in cream and cooled chocolate. Pour mixture into lamington or cake tin, cover with foil, freeze several hours or until mixture begins to set.

Toast almonds on oven tray in moderate oven for about 5 minutes. Combine extra cooled chocolate, almonds and cherries, immediately fold into icy mixture, spread into deep 23cm flan tin, cover with foil; freeze overnight. Remove from tin, cut into wedges, decorate with extra whipped cream and extra cherries if desired.

Serves 6 to 8.

LEFT: Clockwise from top left: Frozen Chocolate Pecan Cake; Frozen Icecream Cheesecake with Warm Marsala Sauce; Chocolate Almond Tortoni with Cherries; Two-Chocolate Icecream Cake.

BAKED BLACKBERRY AND PASSIONFRUIT CHEESECAKE

Cheesecake can be made a day before required if preferred. Use any type of berry in this recipe. Thaw frozen berries before using.

CRUMB CRUST
90g butter, melted
185g packaged sweet biscuits, crushed
FILLING
125g packet cream cheese
¼ cup castor sugar
2 tablespoons lemon juice
2 eggs
300ml carton thickened cream
250g fresh or frozen blackberries
2 passionfruit

Crumb Crust: Combine butter and biscuit crumbs, press evenly over base and side of 23cm flan tin; bake in moderate oven 10 minutes, cool. Spread blackberry mixture over Crust, top with Filling. Place on oven tray, bake in moderate oven 30 minutes or until set. Cool, refrigerate, serve with extra cream and blackberries.

Filling: Have cream cheese at room temperature, place in small bowl with sugar and lemon juice, beat with electric mixer until smooth, beat in eggs one at a time. Add cream, beat until combined. Combine blackberries and passionfruit pulp.

BLACK FOREST BAVAROIS WITH CHOCOLATE SAUCE

We used a Swiss liqueur called Cheri-Suisse to flavor the Sauce; Creme de Cacao would also be delicious.

½ cup castor sugar
3 egg yolks
1 vanilla bean
1½ cups milk
3 teaspoons gelatine
2 tablespoons water
300ml carton thickened cream
425g can black cherries, drained
CHOCOLATE SAUCE
100g dark chocolate, chopped
½ cup cream
2 tablespoons chocolate cherry liqueur

Combine sugar and egg yolks in pan, whisk constantly over low heat until mixture is pale in color; do not allow to boil. Cut a long slit in the vanilla bean. Heat milk and vanilla bean in pan for 10 minutes; do not boil. (This is to extract flavor from the bean.) Strain milk, discard bean. Gradually stir milk into sugar mixture, stir constantly with wooden spoon until custard thickens slightly; do not allow to boil, remove from heat.

Sprinkle gelatine over water, dissolve over hot water (or microwave on HIGH for about 20 seconds). Stir gelatine mixture into custard, place into large bowl, cool to lukewarm. Beat cream until soft peaks form, fold into custard. Pour into 4 individual lightly-oiled moulds (1 cup capacity), place on tray. Refrigerate several hours or overnight. Turn moulds onto plates, serve topped with Sauce and cherries.

Chocolate Sauce: Melt chocolate and cream over hot water, add liqueur, stir until smooth, cool.

Serves 4.

PLUM AND ALMOND TART

PASTRY
1 cup plain flour
90g butter
1 egg yolk
1 tablespoon water, approximately

FILLING
2 x 450g cans plums, drained
1 cup (125g) ground almonds
½ cup castor sugar
2 teaspoons grated lemon rind
1 egg, lightly beaten
30g butter
1 tablespoon castor sugar, extra
2 teaspoons cinnamon

Pastry: Sift flour into bowl, rub in butter. Add egg yolk and enough water to mix to a dry dough. Turn onto lightly floured surface, knead lightly until smooth, cover, refrigerate 30 minutes. Roll pastry large enough to line a 23cm flan tin; refrigerate 30 minutes. Spread almond mixture into Pastry case, top with plums, dot with butter, sprinkle with sugar mixture. Bake in moderate oven for about 50 minutes or until golden brown. Dust with icing sugar, serve warm or cold with whipped cream and flaked almonds.

Filling: Halve and seed plums; drain on absorbent paper. Combine almonds, sugar, lemon rind and egg in bowl, mix to a paste. Combine extra sugar and cinnamon thoroughly.

CARAMEL ALMOND TART

ALMOND PASTRY
90g butter
¼ cup castor sugar
1 egg yolk
1 tablespoon milk
¾ cup plain flour
¼ cup self-raising flour
⅓ cup ground almonds

FILLING
400g can sweetened condensed milk
125g butter
½ teaspoon almond essence
½ cup castor sugar
2 eggs
½ cup plain flour
½ cup ground almonds
⅓ cup slivered almonds

ICING
½ cup icing sugar
1 teaspoon lemon juice, approximately

LEFT: Black Forest Bavarois with Chocolate Sauce.
BELOW: Left to right: Plum and Almond Tart; Caramel Almond Tart; Baked Blackberry and Passionfruit Cheesecake.

Almond Pastry: Cream butter and sugar in small bowl with electric mixer until light and fluffy, beat in egg yolk and milk. Stir in sifted flours and almonds in 2 batches, shape pastry into a ball, cover; refrigerate 30 minutes.

Roll Pastry large enough to line a 23cm flan tin; trim edges. Bake blind by covering Pastry with greaseproof paper and filling tin with dried beans or rice. Bake in moderately hot oven 7 minutes. Remove beans and paper carefully, return to oven, bake further 7 minutes. Spread base of Pastry case with hot condensed milk, spread evenly with Filling, sprinkle with slivered almonds. Bake in moderate oven 30 minutes or until golden brown. Serve cold, drizzled with Icing.

Filling: Place condensed milk into heavy-based pan, stir constantly and briskly over medium heat for about 10 minutes or until milk is a caramel color; cool 15 minutes before using. Cream butter, almond essence and sugar in small bowl with electric mixer until light and fluffy, beat in eggs one at a time. Stir in sifted flour and ground almonds.

Icing: Sift icing sugar into bowl, stir in enough lemon juice to give mixture a pouring consistency.

PEAR AND RUM SORBET WITH LOGANBERRY SAUCE

Make Sorbet and Sauce up to two days ahead if preferred.

⅔ cup sugar
⅔ cup water
825g can pear halves, drained
¼ cup lemon juice
2 tablespoons white rum
LOGANBERRY SAUCE
425g can loganberries
2 teaspoons arrowroot
1 tablespoon lemon juice

Combine sugar and water in pan, stir over heat without boiling until sugar is dissolved. Bring mixture up to the boil, remove from heat immediately; cool, then refrigerate.

Blend or process pears until smooth, add lemon juice, rum and sugar syrup. Pour mixture into freezer trays or lamington tin, cover with foil, freeze several hours or overnight. Serve scoops of Sorbet with Sauce.

Loganberry Sauce: Place undrained loganberries in pan, bring to the boil, stir in blended arrowroot and lemon juice, stir constantly over heat until Sauce boils and thickens, cool; refrigerate before serving.

Serves 4.

BANANA SORBET WITH KIWI FRUIT

⅔ cup sugar
⅔ cup water
2 large ripe bananas
1 cup orange juice
1 tablespoon lemon juice
2 tablespoons brandy
1 kiwi fruit
2 teaspoons sugar, extra

Combine sugar and water in pan, stir over heat without boiling until sugar is dissolved. Bring sugar syrup up to the boil, remove from heat immediately, cool, refrigerate.

Blend or process bananas until smooth, add orange and lemon juice, brandy and sugar syrup; blend until smooth. Pour mixture into lamington tin or freezer trays, cover with foil, freeze several hours or overnight.

Blend or process kiwi fruit with extra sugar, serve over Sorbet.

Serves 6.

BELOW: Back: Banana Sorbet with Kiwi Fruit; front: Pear and Rum Sorbet with Loganberry Sauce.
RIGHT: Back: White Chocolate Cases with Icecream and Apricot Sauce; front: Strawberry and Passionfruit Icecream Victoria.

WHITE CHOCOLATE CASES WITH ICECREAM AND APRICOT SAUCE

Foil pie trays can be bought from kitchenware stores. Chocolate cases will keep, covered, in refrigerator for about a month. Apricot Sauce can be made up to four days ahead. We used commercially made icecream.

250g white chocolate, melted.
APRICOT SAUCE
½ cup chopped dried apricots
1 cup water
2 tablespoons sugar
¼ teaspoon cinnamon

Using a teaspoon, spread chocolate evenly over base and sides of 4 individual foil pie trays (base measures 7cm); make top edge as even as possible; refrigerate until set. Carefully pull foil trays away from chocolate, serve icecream in chocolate cases, topped with Sauce, fruit and a little extra grated white chocolate if desired.

Apricot Sauce: Combine all ingredients in pan, bring to the boil, reduce heat, simmer, covered, 5 minutes or until apricots have softened (or microwave on HIGH about 4 minutes), cool; blend or process until smooth.

Serves 4.

STRAWBERRY AND PASSIONFRUIT ICECREAM VICTORIA

You will need to use about six large passionfruit for this recipe.

2 x 250g punnets strawberries
2 tablespoons icing sugar
½ cup passionfruit pulp
STRAWBERRY AND
PASSIONFRUIT ICECREAM
3 egg yolks
¾ cup castor sugar
1 cup milk
250g punnet strawberries
¼ cup passionfruit pulp
2 x 300ml cartons thickened cream
red food coloring

Halve strawberries. Add icing sugar and passionfruit, serve with Icecream.

Strawberry and Passionfruit Icecream: Beat egg yolks and sugar in small bowl with electric mixer until thick and creamy. Heat milk in pan until just below boiling point, reduce heat, gradually stir in egg yolk mixture, stir over low heat, without boiling, until mixture thickens slightly; cool to room temperature. Divide between 2 bowls.

Blend or process strawberries until smooth; you will need ⅔ cup puree for this recipe. Add strawberry puree and 1 carton of cream to 1 bowl of custard; tint pink with a little coloring. Stir passionfruit and remaining carton of cream into remaining custard; mix well. Fold the 2 mixtures together to give a marbled effect. Pour into freezer trays or cake tin, cover with foil, freeze overnight.

Serves 6.

AMARETTO ZABAGLIONE WITH PEACHES AND ORANGE

Use canned peaches if fresh peaches are out of season. Amaretto is an almond-flavored liqueur.

6 ripe peaches, peeled
2 tablespoons orange juice
4 egg yolks
1 tablespoon sugar
½ cup Amaretto
1 cup sugar, extra
1 cup (125g) blanched almonds
300ml carton thickened cream

Slice peaches, place in bowl, add orange juice. Combine egg yolks and sugar in top of double boiler over simmering water. Beat with rotary beater or electric mixer until pale in color, gradually beat in Amaretto, beat constantly until mixture is thick; transfer to large bowl, cool to room temperature.

Combine extra sugar and almonds in heavy pan, cook over heat until sugar begins to turn brown, stir gently until sugar is dissolved and golden brown. Pour toffee onto greased oven tray; cool. Break almond toffee roughly, blend or process until coarsely crushed; whip cream until soft peaks form; stir in ½ cup of the almond toffee, fold into Amaretto mixture. Serve over peaches, sprinkled with some of the remaining toffee.

Reserve any remaining toffee in jar for another use.

Serves 6.

FRESH FRUIT SHORTCAKES

Use any fresh fruit for this recipe.

2 cups plain flour
185g butter
½ cup icing sugar
1 egg yolk
300ml carton thickened cream
1 tablespoon Grand Marnier
1 teaspoon grated orange rind

Sift flour into bowl, rub in cold chopped butter, mix in sifted icing sugar, egg yolk and 2 tablespoons of the cream; mix to a soft dough. Knead lightly until smooth, cover, refrigerate 30 minutes. Divide mixture evenly into 8; roll out each piece to 8cm circle. Pinch a decorative edge with floured fingers. Place Shortcakes on lightly greased oven trays; bake them in a moderate oven 20 minutes or until pale golden brown.

Beat remaining cream until soft peaks form, stir in Grand Marnier and orange rind. Top Shortcakes with cream mixture, then with fruit.

Serves 8.

MARINATED FRESH FRUIT WITH CREME FRAICHE

Choose any combination of fresh summer fruit for this recipe. Prepare Creme Fraiche two to seven days before required if preferred. Cointreau is an orange-flavored liqueur.

2 mangoes, sliced
2 kiwi fruit, sliced
250g punnet strawberries
¼ cup Cointreau
CREME FRAICHE
300ml carton thickened cream
3 tablespoons buttermilk

Halve strawberries, combine all fruit in bowl, add Cointreau, cover; refrigerate several hours or overnight. Serve with Creme Fraiche.

Creme Fraiche: Combine cream and buttermilk in bowl, whisk until smooth, cover, stand at room temperature for about 24 hours or until mixture is thick; time will depend on room temperature. Refrigerate until serving time.

Serves 4.

IRISH COFFEE ICECREAM

4 egg yolks
¾ cup castor sugar
2 x 300ml cartons thickened cream
3 teaspoons instant coffee powder
2 tablespoons hot water
⅓ cup Irish whiskey

Beat egg yolks and sugar in small bowl with electric mixer until light and fluffy. Heat cream in pan until almost boiling. While mixer is operating, gradually beat in cream in a thin stream, then beat in combined coffee and water, then whiskey. Pour into lamington tin or freezer trays, cover with foil; freeze for several hours or until partly frozen.

Chop icecream roughly, return to small bowl of mixer, beat until smooth, return to lamington tin, cover with foil; freeze until set. Serve with fruit and whipped cream if desired.

Serves 4.

LEFT: Top: Amaretto Zabaglione with Peaches and Orange; centre: Fresh Fruit Shortcakes; bottom: Marinated Fresh Fruit with Creme Fraiche.
RIGHT: Irish Coffee Icecream.

MERINGUE NESTS WITH RASPBERRY MOUSSE

"Nests" can be made a week ahead if preferred; store in airtight container. Use any type of berry in this recipe. Thaw frozen berries before use.

4 egg whites
1¼ cups castor sugar
2 teaspoons cornflour
1 teaspoon white vinegar
½ teaspoon vanilla
RASPBERRY MOUSSE
2 eggs, separated
⅓ cup castor sugar
¼ cup milk
250g fresh or frozen raspberries
3 teaspoons gelatine
2 tablespoons water
300ml carton thickened cream

Combine egg whites, sugar, cornflour, vinegar and vanilla in small bowl of electric mixer, beat on high speed for 15 minutes or until mixture is thick and sugar completely dissolved. Place mixture into piping bag fitted with large fluted tube. Pipe "nests" about 8cm in diameter onto greased and cornfloured oven trays; allow room for spreading. Sides of "nests": should be at least 3cm high. Bake in very slow oven 1¼ hours or until crisp and dry. Turn oven off, cool in oven. Place "nests" onto serving plates, fill with Mousse just before serving. Serve with extra whipped cream and extra raspberries if desired.

Raspberry Mousse: Combine egg yolks, sugar and milk in pan, stir over low heat until slightly thickened, do not allow to boil; remove from heat. Blend or process raspberries until smooth, add to egg yolk mixture. Sprinkle gelatine over water, dissolve over hot water (or microwave on HIGH for about 30 seconds); stir into raspberry mixture; transfer to large bowl, cool to room temperature. Beat cream until soft peaks form, fold into raspberry mixture. Beat egg whites until soft peaks form, fold into raspberry mixture.

Serves 6.

LIQUEUR DOUBLE INDULGENCE CHOCOLATE MOUSSE

Mousse can be made the day before required, covered and refrigerated.

125g dark chocolate, melted
1 tablespoon Tia Maria or Kahlua
4 eggs, separated
3 teaspoons gelatine
2 tablespoons water
300ml carton thickened cream
CHOCOLATE TOPPING
125g dark chocolate, chopped
30g butter

HOT CHOCOLATE BROWNIE SOUFFLES WITH RUM SAUCE

90g butter
2 tablespoons plain flour
125g dark chocolate, melted
½ cup sugar
1 tablespoon instant coffee powder
1 tablespoon rum
1 teaspoon vanilla
4 eggs, separated
RUM SAUCE
2 cups vanilla icecream
2 tablespoons rum

Grease 6 individual souffle dishes (½ cup capacity), sprinkle lightly with sugar. Melt butter in pan, stir in flour, cook over heat 1 minute, stirring constantly. Add chocolate, sugar and blended coffee, rum and vanilla; stir constantly over heat until smooth, do not boil. Remove from heat, quickly stir in egg yolks. Transfer mixture to a large bowl. Beat egg whites until soft peaks form, fold lightly into chocolate mixture. Pour into dishes, place dishes on oven tray, bake in moderate oven for about 15 minutes. Sift icing sugar over souffles, serve immediately with cold Sauce.

Rum Sauce: Soften icecream at room temperature for about 10 minutes, stir in rum, beat until smooth.

Serves 6.

ABOVE: Hot Chocolate Brownie Souffles with Rum Sauce.
RIGHT: Top: Liqueur Double Indulgence Chocolate Mousse; bottom left: Rhubarb Mousse with Strawberry Glaze; right: Meringue Nests with Raspberry Mousse.

Cool chocolate for a few minutes, gradually stir in combined Tia Maria and egg yolks. Sprinkle gelatine over water, dissolve over hot water (or microwave on HIGH about 40 seconds), cool 10 minutes, stir into chocolate mixture. Beat cream until soft peaks form, fold into chocolate mixture. Beat egg whites in small bowl with electric mixer until soft peaks form, fold into chocolate mixture, pour into lightly oiled, round 20cm cake or sandwich tin, cover; refrigerate until set. Turn Mousse onto serving plate. Place a piece of plastic wrap onto flat surface, spread Topping evenly into a 25cm circle. Invert plastic over top of Mousse, press down lightly over side of Mousse; refrigerate until Topping is set. Carefully remove plastic wrap, cut Mousse into wedges to serve. Serve with extra cream and fruit if desired.

Chocolate Topping: Melt chocolate and butter over hot water, stir until smooth before using.

RHUBARB MOUSSE WITH STRAWBERRY GLAZE

Fresh or frozen rhubarb can be used for this recipe. If individual flans are not available, moulds of three-quarter cup capacity can be used. If using metal flan tins the rhubarb mixture can cause them to discolor; turn Mousse from the flan tins as soon as they are set.

4 cups (400g) chopped rhubarb
¾ cup water
¼ cup sugar
250g punnet strawberries
1 tablespoon gelatine
3 tablespoons water
2 egg whites
¼ cup sugar, extra
STRAWBERRY GLAZE
250g punnet strawberries
¼ cup sugar
red food coloring

Combine rhubarb, water and sugar in pan, bring to the boil, reduce heat, cover, cook about 5 minutes or until rhubarb is tender; blend or process with strawberries until smooth. Sprinkle gelatine over water, dissolve over hot water (or microwave on HIGH about 40 seconds), add to rhubarb mixture; cool to room temperature.

Beat egg whites in small bowl with electric mixer until soft peaks form, gradually add extra sugar, beat until dissolved, fold into rhubarb mixture. Pour mixture into 6 lightly oiled, deep 8cm flan tins, refrigerate several hours until set. Turn onto serving plates, spread with Glaze.

Strawberry Glaze: Blend or process strawberries and sugar until smooth. Pour into pan, tint pink with a drop or two of food coloring. Stir over heat until thick and reduced by about half; cool to room temperature.

Serves 6.

CHAMPAGNE AND ORANGE LIQUEUR JELLIES

Creme de Cassis is a blackcurrant-flavored liqueur; any fruit-flavored liqueur of your choice would be delightful in this recipe.

3 teaspoons gelatine
2 tablespoons water
½ cup sugar
⅓ cup orange juice, strained
2 cups champagne
1 tablespoon Creme de Cassis

Sprinkle gelatine over water, dissolve over hot water (or microwave on HIGH about 20 seconds). Combine gelatine mixture, sugar and orange juice in pan, stir over low heat without boiling until sugar is dissolved. Remove from heat, cool 5 minutes, add champagne and liqueur, stir gently until bubbles subside. Pour mixture into 6 individual serving glasses, cover, refrigerate several hours or overnight. Serve with fruit or whipped cream if desired.

Serves 6.

LIQUEUR JELLY JEWELS

Make up to one day ahead. Creme de Menthe is a mint-flavored liqueur.

2 x 100g packets lemon jelly crystals
2 cups boiling water
1 cup dry white wine
2 tablespoons Grand Marnier
1 tablespoon Creme de Menthe
red food coloring
blue food coloring

Place jelly crystals in bowl, add water, stir until crystals are dissolved, stir in wine. Divide jelly evenly into 3 bowls, add Grand Marnier to 1 bowl and tint red with a little coloring. Add Creme de Menthe to another bowl and tint to green using a little blue coloring.

Divide the green jelly evenly into 4 glasses; refrigerate until set. Gently pour in yellow jelly; refrigerate until set. Gently pour in red jelly, refrigerate until set. Serve topped with whipped cream.

Serves 4.

MOCHA RASPBERRY TRIFLE

Any berry of your choice can be used in this recipe; thaw frozen berries well before using.

2 x 225g Chocolate Sponge Rolls
⅓ cup Tia Maria or Kahlua
500g fresh or frozen raspberries
100g dark chocolate, grated
300ml carton thickened cream
COFFEE CUSTARD
4 egg yolks
¼ cup cornflour
¾ cup castor sugar
1½ cups milk
1 tablespoon instant coffee powder
1 tablespoon hot water
2 teaspoons vanilla
300ml carton thickened cream

Cut rolls into 8 slices. Place half the slices over base of serving dish. Sprinkle evenly with half the Tia Maria, top with half the raspberries, sprinkle with one-third of the chocolate, spread with half the Custard. Repeat layers. Decorate with whipped cream, remaining chocolate and extra raspberries.

Coffee Custard: Whisk egg yolks, cornflour and sugar together in pan until smooth. Heat milk in separate pan, gradually stir into egg yolk mixture. Cook, stirring constantly, until mixture boils and thickens. Add combined coffee, water and vanilla, cover surface with plastic wrap to prevent skin forming; cool to room temperature. Beat cream until soft peaks form, fold into the Custard.

Serves 8.

LAYERED COFFEE CREAM

Make this dessert the day before required. We used slender Lady Finger Biscuits; Savoiardi sponge fingers can also be used.

250g packet cream cheese
4 eggs, separated
¼ cup castor sugar
½ cup sour cream
2 teaspoons vanilla
1 tablespoon instant coffee powder
1 tablespoon castor sugar, extra
2 cups hot water
200g packet Lady Finger Biscuits

LEFT: Back: Champagne and Orange Liqueur Jellies; front: Liqueur Jelly Jewels.
ABOVE: Back: Mocha Raspberry Trifle; front: Layered Coffee Cream.

Have cream cheese at room temperature. Beat egg yolks and sugar together in small bowl with electric mixer until pale and creamy. Add chopped cream cheese, sour cream and vanilla, beat until smooth; transfer to large bowl. Beat egg whites until soft peaks form, fold into cream cheese mixture. Combine coffee, extra sugar and hot water in bowl, stir until dissolved. Dip biscuits into coffee mixture one at a time for a few seconds, and place a layer of the biscuits into a serving dish. Pour half the cream cheese mixture over biscuits, top with another layer of biscuits dipped in coffee mixture; pour remaining cream cheese mixture over biscuits. Top with another layer of biscuits dipped in coffee mixture; refrigerate overnight. Decorate with cream and chocolate curls and dust with sifted cocoa.

Serves 6.

COLD RASPBERRY SOUFFLES

Any type of fresh or frozen berry can be used for this recipe.

500g fresh or frozen raspberries
4 eggs, separated
⅔ cup castor sugar
½ cup milk
1 tablespoon gelatine
¼ cup water
2 x 300ml cartons thickened cream

Blend or process thawed raspberries, strain to remove seeds. Whisk egg yolks and sugar together in pan, over low heat until pale in color, whisk in milk, cook, stirring, with wooden spoon, until the custard thickens slightly; do not allow to boil. Add raspberry puree, cool to room temperature. Sprinkle gelatine over water, dissolve over hot water, cool to room temperature (do not allow to set); stir into raspberry mixture. Beat cream until firm peaks form, fold in raspberry mixture in 2 lots. Beat egg whites until firm peaks form, fold into raspberry mixture.

Place a collar of foil around 6 individual dishes (½ cup capacity), secure foil with string. Brush inside of foil very lightly with oil. Pour raspberry mixture into the dishes; refrigerate several hours or overnight. Cut string, remove foil collars. Decorate Souffles with extra whipped cream, raspberries and chocolate curls if desired.

Serves 6.

FRESH FIG MOUSSE

2 tablespoons sugar
2 tablespoons plain flour
⅔ cup milk
2 egg yolks
½ cup sugar, extra
⅓ cup dry white wine
8 fresh figs, peeled, chopped
3 teaspoons gelatine
2 tablespoons water
½ cup thickened cream
red food coloring

Mix sugar and flour together in pan, gradually blend in combined milk and egg yolks, stir until smooth. Stir constantly over heat until mixture boils and thickens; cool to room temperature.

Place extra sugar, wine and figs in pan, bring to the boil, reduce heat, cover, simmer 5 minutes; cool to room temperature. Sprinkle gelatine over water, dissolve over hot water (or microwave on HIGH about 20 seconds). Blend or process egg mixture and fig mixture until smooth, add gelatine mixture, process until combined. Transfer to large bowl, fold in whipped cream, tint pale pink with food coloring, spoon into serving glasses, refrigerate several hours or overnight. Serve with extra whipped cream and extra figs if desired.

Serves 6.

PASSIONFRUIT MOUSSE WITH MANGO COULIS

You will need about six large passionfruit for this recipe.

3 teaspoons gelatine
2 tablespoons water
¾ cup passionfruit pulp
½ cup thickened cream
¼ cup castor sugar
2 tablespoons lemon juice
MANGO COULIS
1 mango, chopped
¼ cup sugar
¼ cup water
1 tablespoon lemon juice

Sprinkle gelatine over water, dissolve over hot water (or microwave on HIGH for about 20 seconds), cool. Combine passionfruit, cream, sugar and lemon juice in bowl. Add gelatine to passionfruit mixture. Lightly oil 6 egg rings, place on serving plates, pour passionfruit mixture into egg rings; refrigerate several hours. Remove rings, serve with Coulis and fresh fruit.

Mango Coulis: Combine mango in pan with sugar and water, bring to the boil, reduce heat, simmer uncovered 2 minutes; cool. Blend or process until smooth, add lemon juice.

Serves 6.

BELOW: Cold Raspberry Souffles.
RIGHT: Back: Fresh Fig Mousse; front: Passionfruit Mousse with Mango Coulis.

SIZZLING SUCCESSES

Making the most of the Australian summer means making the most of our outdoor entertaining opportunities . . . on boats, on beaches or in the backyard. Barbecues, the ultimate salute to our relaxed lifestyle, can be as easy or as festive as you like; the sauces and imaginative salads are the special effects for popular stand-bys like steak and sausages. The recipes in this section are enough to serve 10 people; mix and match the recipes for a fresh approach each time.

RADISHES WITH MUSTARD AND LEMON MAYONNAISE
3 bunches radishes
2 egg yolks
½ cup oil
1 tablespoon seeded mustard
1 tablespoon lemon juice
black pepper
Trim radishes, place in bowl, cover with water, refrigerate several hours to make radishes crisp. Place egg yolks in bowl, whisk well, add oil drop by drop, beating well after each addition until thick and creamy (this can be done in a blender or processor). Stir in mustard, lemon juice and pepper. Serve with drained radishes.

SAUCY CHICKEN WINGS

Bake the day before if preferred and reheat on the barbecue.

1½kg (about 20) chicken wings
¼ cup dry sherry
2 tablespoons tomato sauce
2 tablespoons barbecue sauce
few drops tabasco sauce
2 tablespoons honey

Remove tips from wings. Cut chicken wings in half at the joint. Combine sherry in large baking dish with sauces and honey, mix in chicken. Place chicken in single layer in dish, bake in moderate oven 1 hour, basting occasionally. Reheat cooked chicken on barbecue before serving.

CREAMY AVOCADO DIP

Can be made several hours before serving; keep tightly covered.

1 avocado
300g carton sour cream
½ cup grated tasty cheese
¼ teaspoon chilli powder
2 teaspoons lemon juice

Blend or process all ingredients until smooth, cover, refrigerate until serving. Serve with savory biscuits and fresh vegetables.

Clockwise from right: Creamy Avocado Dip; Marinated Olives; Radishes with Mustard and Lemon Mayonnaise; Saucy Chicken Wings.

MARINATED OLIVES

These olives can be prepared weeks ahead. After using, reserve the oil mixture and replenish jar with more olives.

250g black olives
250g green olives
½ cup olive oil
½ cup oil
¼ cup lemon juice
2 cloves garlic, crushed
2 tablespoons chopped parsley
2 tablespoons chopped fresh dill
1 small fresh chilli, finely chopped

Cut several small slits in each olive, combine in jar with remaining ingredients, cover, marinate several days before using.

CURRIED SOUR CREAM POTATOES

Potatoes can be partly cooked in a moderate oven 45 minutes, then placed in barbecue coals for remaining half of the cooking time.

10 large old potatoes
⅓ cup oil
1 tablespoon salt
2 x 300g cartons sour cream
2 teaspoons curry powder
2 tablespoons fruit chutney
4 green shallots, finely chopped

Pierce potatoes all over with skewer, brush with oil, rub with salt. Wrap potatoes individually in foil, place into coals of barbecue or bake about 1 to 1½ hours. Cut a deep cross through foil and into potato. Using a cloth, hold potato around the middle, squeeze gently to open out. Top potatoes with combined sour cream, curry and chutney, sprinkle with shallots before serving.

FRESH CORN ON THE COB WITH GARLIC BUTTER

10 fresh corn cobs
185g butter
2 cloves garlic, crushed

Have butter at room temperature. Remove silks from corn, peel husks; do not remove husks. Beat butter and garlic together. Spread each corn cob with garlic butter, enclose each cob with husks. Wrap each cob in foil. Barbecue or bake for about 30 minutes or until tender, turning often.

MARINATED ONION RINGS

10 onions, thickly sliced
¼ cup dried black peppercorns
1 cup oil
1 tablespoon paprika
2 teaspoons sugar
fresh rosemary sprigs

Blend or grind peppercorns coarsely. Place oil in shallow dish, stir in pepper, paprika, sugar and rosemary. Add onion rings, cover, marinate several hours or overnight. Cook onions on barbecue plate or in pan, add marinade a little at a time to help brown onions during cooking.

KUMARA AND POTATO SALAD

Kumara is an orange-colored sweet potato. Make salad the day before if preferred.

1kg (about 4) kumara
1kg (about 6) potatoes
30g butter
2 onions, chopped
2 bacon rashers
2 cloves garlic, crushed
2 tablespoons chopped fresh basil
½ cup French dressing
½ cup sour cream
5 hard-boiled eggs, chopped

Cut peeled kumara and potatoes into chips, place into pan, cover with water, bring to the boil, reduce heat, simmer 10 minutes or until just tender; do not overcook; drain; cool.

Heat butter in pan, add onions and bacon, cook, stirring, few minutes or until onions are soft; add garlic and basil, pour into bowl. Stir in dressing and sour cream, then gently fold in kumara, potatoes and eggs; refrigerate, covered, until ready to serve.

SEASONED TURKEY COOKED IN A SALT CRUST

Long cooking and total enclosure in a hard salt crust will ensure the turkey is moist and tender. The large quantity of salt is necessary to ensure that the crust becomes rock hard during the cooking. Because the turkey is wrapped in foil, it will not come in contact with the salt. We cooked the turkey in two large disposable foil baking trays; these are available from kitchenware stores.

3kg turkey
1½ cups stale breadcrumbs
1 onion, chopped
½ cup sultanas
2 tablespoons fruit chutney
1 teaspoon curry powder
1 egg, lightly beaten
¼ cup tomato sauce
¼ cup Worcestershire sauce
2 teaspoons French mustard
SALT CRUST
2kg cooking salt
8 cups plain flour
1 litre (4 cups) water, approximately

Cut turkey in half along the breast bone, remove excess fat. Combine breadcrumbs, onion, sultanas, chutney, curry and egg; press into cavity of each turkey half. Combine sauces with mustard, brush over turkey skin. Wrap each half tightly in well-oiled foil. Divide Salt Crust in half, roll each half out to a rectangle, about 40cm x 50cm. Place turkey, breast side up, in centre, fold Crust over turkey to completely enclose it, press edges together. Using wet hands, smooth out all joins to ensure there are no gaps for the steam to escape. Place turkey halves into 2 baking trays, cover with foil, place directly onto coals or barbecue plate, or bake in moderately slow oven for 3 hours. To serve turkey, break crust with mallet or hammer, be careful of steam. Salt Crust is not meant to be eaten.
Salt Crust: Sift flour and salt into a large bowl, stir in enough water to make a firm but pliable dough.

SHREDDED LETTUCE SALAD WITH TANGY LEMON DRESSING
1 lettuce, finely shredded
1 onion, thinly sliced
1 cucumber, thinly sliced
250g punnet cherry tomatoes
TANGY LEMON DRESSING
½ cup oil
¼ cup lemon juice
1 tablespoon sugar
2 tablespoons chopped parsley
2 tablespoons chopped mint
Combine all ingredients in large bowl, add Dressing before serving, toss well.
Tangy Lemon Dressing: Combine all ingredients in jar; shake well.

ABOVE: Back: Shredded Lettuce Salad with Tangy Lemon Dressing; front, from left: Seasoned Turkey Cooked in a Salt Crust; Kumara and Potato Salad.
LEFT: Back, from left: Curried Sour Cream Potatoes; Fresh Corn on the Cob with Garlic Butter; front: Marinated Onion Rings.

LAMB ON A SPIT GIVES THE GRAND TOUCH TO A BARBECUE

Many home barbecues have a spit attachment, but it is inexpensive to hire one. The flavor from home-roasted lamb is quite exceptional and it is an easy, economical way to entertain a lot of people.

One lamb will easily serve 20 people, although this depends on your guests' appetites, and what else you are serving at the barbecue. There are a few rules to follow for failproof results. As a guide, a 15kg lamb will take about 4 hours to cook; add another hour for each additional 5kg.

It is important that the lamb be at room temperature before cooking. This could take about 12 hours, depending on the storage temperature and room temperature. Always have the fire lit at least an hour before the lamb is put on the spit. Concentrate the fire towards both ends of the lamb; the rib area needs to cook more slowly than these thicker parts. Keep the fire replenished during the cooking.

Before the lamb is placed on the spit, remove any fat, particularly from the kidney area.

You will need someone to help place the lamb on the spit; make sure it is as well-balanced as possible. Tie the neck onto the spit with wire. If it does not sit securely, make a slit in the neck. "Sew" the chest and stomach cavities together with wire.

You will need to brush the lamb with a Baster before it is cooked; no more basting is necessary during the cooking. After slicing the meat, splash a little of the Baster over the cut surface on the lamb; this helps retain moisture. Choose the Baster you prefer.

Lamb can be carved while it is still on the spit. Alternatively lamb can be removed from the spit (you will need help) and chopped into pieces to serve.

LEMON BASTER
2 cups strained lemon juice
1 cup water
1 tablespoon salt
Combine all ingredients.

SWEET AND SOUR BASTER
¼ cup oil
¼ cup Worcestershire sauce
1 cup brown vinegar
1 cup water
½ cup brown sugar
½ cup tomato sauce
2 tablespoons tomato paste
Combine all ingredients.

BACON-WRAPPED SAUSAGES
10 thick sausages
10 bacon rashers
¼ cup plum sauce
1 teaspoon curry powder
Place sausages into pan of cold water, cover, bring up to the boil, drain, cool. Wrap a rasher of bacon around each sausage, secure with toothpicks. Brush sausages with combined plum sauce and curry powder. Barbecue or grill until sausages are cooked through and bacon crisp, brush occasionally during cooking with any remaining plum sauce mixture.

MIXED RICE SALAD WITH CREAMY TOMATO DRESSING
1 cup brown rice
1 cup white rice
4 bacon rashers, chopped
2 onions, chopped
3 cups (375g) frozen corn and peas
1 cup sultanas
CREAMY TOMATO DRESSING
½ cup oil
¼ cup white vinegar
2 tablespoons mayonnaise
2 tablespoons tomato sauce
2 cloves garlic, crushed
Add brown rice to large pan of rapidly boiling water, boil rapidly uncovered for 15 minutes, add white rice, boil further 15 minutes or until rice is tender; drain, cool.

Add bacon and onions to pan, cook, stirring, until onions are soft and bacon crisp; drain. Boil, steam or microwave corn and peas until tender; drain; rinse under cold water; drain. Combine all ingredients in bowl with Dressing.
Creamy Tomato Dressing: Combine all ingredients in jar; shake well.

THREE BEAN SALAD

The imported kidney and broad beans we used in this salad are available at delicatessens; any dried or canned bean of your choice can be used.

3 x 432g cans kidney beans
3 x 310g cans butter beans
3 x 283g cans broad beans
¼ cup chopped parsley
½ cup French dressing
¼ cup sour cream
1 tablespoon seeded mustard
Drain beans, rinse well under cold water; drain well. Combine parsley in bowl with dressing, sour cream and mustard; mix in beans.

MARINATED HONEYED HAM AND CHICKEN STICKS

If using wooden skewers, soak them in water for several hours or overnight before using; this prevents them burning during cooking. Chicken and ham can be marinated up to two days before cooking if preferred.

6 chicken breast fillets
500g leg ham
MARINADE
⅓ cup honey
⅓ cup oil
2 tablespoons Worcestershire sauce
1 tablespoon grated orange rind
2 cloves garlic, crushed
Cut chicken fillets and ham into long strips, add to Marinade, cover, refrigerate at least 1 hour. Thread meat onto skewers. Cook on hot barbecue plate or grill until browned and cooked through; turn occasionally, brushing with Marinade during cooking.
Marinade: Combine all ingredients.
Makes about 20.

MUSTARD SAUSAGES WITH SMOKED OYSTERS
10 thick sausages
2 x 105g cans smoked oysters, drained
1 tablespoon lemon juice
2 tablespoons French mustard
1 teaspoon sugar
Place sausages in pan of cold water, cover, bring up to the boil; drain, cool. Cut sausages half way through centre lengthways, fill cavity with oysters, secure opening with toothpicks. Brush sausages with combined lemon juice, mustard and sugar, barbecue or grill until sausages are cooked through.

Back: Mustard Sausages with Smoked Oysters; Bacon-Wrapped Sausages; centre: Mixed Rice Salad with Creamy Tomato Dressing; front, from left: Marinated Honeyed Ham and Chicken Sticks; Three Bean Salad.

SWEET PINEAPPLE COLESLAW

½ cabbage, shredded
6 carrots, grated
6 zucchini, grated
30g butter
¼ cup honey
850g can pineapple pieces, drained
¼ cup chopped parsley
DRESSING
440g can sweetened condensed milk
1 cup white vinegar
2 teaspoons dry mustard

Combine cabbage, carrots and zucchini in bowl. Heat butter in pan, add honey and pineapple, stir constantly over high heat until pineapple is lightly browned, stir into cabbage mixture with parsley and Dressing.
Dressing: Combine all ingredients.

BEETROOT IN GINGER SYRUP

Beetroot can be stored in refrigerator for several weeks.

10 beetroot
½ cup white vinegar
3 cups sugar
1 cup water
2 tablespoons grated fresh ginger
2 teaspoons grated lemon rind
¼ cup lemon juice
1 teaspoon grated orange rind
¼ cup orange juice
2 green shallots, chopped

Boil or steam beetroot until tender; drain, peel, cut into quarters if large. Combine vinegar, sugar, water, ginger, lemon rind and juice and orange rind and juice in pan, stir over heat without boiling until sugar is dissolved. Add beetroot, simmer gently for about 10 minutes; cool. Serve cold sprinkled with shallots.

BARBECUED PORK SPARE RIBS

Request from the butcher, chopped American-style pork spare ribs for this recipe, or use pork rashers. Ribs can be cooked the day before if desired. Bake in a single layer in a large baking dish, basting occasionally, in a moderate oven for 45 minutes or until they are golden brown and tender. Reheat on the barbecue just before serving.

5kg pork spare ribs
1 cup oil
½ cup lemon juice
⅓ cup Worcestershire sauce
2 cloves garlic, crushed
⅓ cup brown sugar
2 teaspoons dry mustard
1 cup fruit chutney

Combine oil in large dish with lemon juice, Worcestershire sauce, garlic, brown sugar, mustard and chutney, brush mixture all over ribs. Stand several hours or refrigerate, covered, overnight. Barbecue ribs until golden brown and cooked through, brushing often with marinade during cooking.

SPICY TOMATO BARBECUE SAUCE

This is a Sauce to make when tomatoes are plentiful; it is delicious and ideal to serve with any type of meat.

1½kg firm ripe tomatoes, chopped
2 onions, chopped
2 apples, chopped
5cm piece fresh ginger, peeled, chopped
1½ cups brown vinegar
1½ cups brown sugar, lightly packed
½ teaspoon cayenne pepper
1 tablespoon Worcestershire sauce
1 teaspoon ground cinnamon
1 teaspoon mixed spice
1 teaspoon ground nutmeg
¼ cup plain flour
2 teaspoons turmeric
¼ cup water

Combine tomatoes, onions and apples in large pan with ginger, vinegar, sugar, pepper, sauce and spices. Stir over heat without boiling until sugar is dissolved, bring to the boil, reduce heat, simmer covered for 2 hours, cool.

Blend or process tomato mixture in batches until smooth; return to pan, simmer uncovered for about 20 minutes. Blend flour and turmeric with water, gradually stir into tomato mixture. Bring to the boil, stirring constantly, until mixture boils and thickens; reduce heat, simmer covered for 30 minutes, or until Sauce is thick. Pour into hot sterilized jars, seal when cold. Store in cool dark place. Store opened jars in refrigerator.

Makes about 1½ litres.

QUICK BARBECUE SAUCE
¼ cup oil
1 onion, chopped
¾ cup tomato sauce
¼ cup water
¼ cup lemon juice
¼ cup Worcestershire sauce
¼ cup brown sugar
2 tablespoons French mustard

Heat oil in pan, add onion, cook, stirring, 2 minutes, add remaining ingredients, bring to the boil, reduce heat, simmer uncovered for 15 minutes or until Sauce is slightly thickened.
    Makes about 1 cup.

SWEET AND SOUR SAUCE

This Sauce can be used immediately.

½ cup honey
½ cup orange juice
¼ cup lemon juice
¼ cup light soy sauce
¼ cup white vinegar
1 clove garlic, crushed
2 teaspoons grated fresh ginger

Combine all ingredients thoroughly.
    Makes about 1½ cups.

MARINATED BABY MUSHROOMS
1kg baby mushrooms
1 tablespoon olive oil
2 cloves garlic, crushed
⅓ cup olive oil, extra
1 tablespoon lemon juice
2 tablespoons chopped parsley
½ teaspoon mixed herbs

Place mushrooms into bowl. Heat oil in pan, add garlic, cook 30 seconds, add remaining ingredients to pan, mix well, pour over mushrooms, cover; refrigerate several hours or overnight.

LEFT: From left: Barbecued Pork Spare Ribs; Sweet Pineapple Coleslaw; Beetroot in Ginger Syrup.
BELOW: Clockwise from front left: Spicy Tomato Barbecue Sauce; Marinated Baby Mushrooms; Quick Barbecue Sauce; Sweet and Sour Sauce.

HOT BREAD WITH FOUR BUTTERS

Use 250g butter (at room temperature) for each variety of butter. This quantity of butter is enough for one long French loaf or two smaller ones. Add ingredients for each variety to chopped butter in electric mixer or processor; beat or process until combined. Butters can be made ahead and refrigerated for up to two weeks, or wrapped securely and kept in freezer for up to three months.

ROSEMARY AND GARLIC
1 teaspoon ground rosemary
1 teaspoon dried mixed herbs
4 cloves garlic, crushed

CHEESE AND CHIVE
1 cup grated tasty cheese
⅓ cup chopped chives

CURRY
1 tablespoon curry powder
2 teaspoons Worcestershire sauce

MUSTARD
⅓ cup seeded mustard

Cut slices into bread at 2cm intervals; be careful not to cut all the way through. Butter both sides of slices generously with the butter of your choice. Wrap bread securely in foil, cook on barbecue plate for about 20 minutes, or bake in moderately hot oven 15 minutes until heated through.

PAN-BARBECUED DAMPERS

Damper can be made and refrigerated for up to four hours before cooking.

PUMPKIN AND BACON DAMPER
375g chopped pumpkin
1 egg, lightly beaten
1 tablespoon milk
2 bacon rashers, chopped
1 onion, chopped
2½ cups self-raising flour
¼ teaspoon cayenne pepper
1 teaspoon dry mustard
60g butter

Boil, steam or microwave pumpkin until tender; drain, push through a sieve. (You should have 1 cup mashed pumpkin.) Stir in egg and milk. Cook bacon and onion in pan until lightly browned, remove from heat. Sift flour, pepper and mustard into bowl, rub in butter, add bacon and onion. Stir in pumpkin mixture. Turn onto lightly floured surface, knead lightly until smooth. Press out to about 3cm thickness with hand, place dough into large, greased, heavy-based shallow pan or place directly onto greased barbecue plate. Using a sharp knife, mark into wedges 1cm deep. Place pan on barbecue plate, cook over medium heat until damper is cooked through; this will take about 30 minutes; turn damper several times during the cooking. Serve hot with butter.

POTATO AND CHEESE DAMPER
Substitute about 2 potatoes for pumpkin, cook and sieve potatoes as for pumpkin, adding an extra ¼ cup milk, ¼ cup grated parmesan cheese, ¼ cup chopped chives and 2 teaspoons dried basil leaves with the potato; proceed as in recipe above.

ABOVE RIGHT: From left: Sherried Cheesecake Trifle; Coffee Meringue Roll with Chocolate Sauce; Mango and Passionfruit Cream Crumble.
LEFT: Back, from left: Potato and Cheese Damper; Pumpkin and Bacon Damper; front: Hot Bread with Four Butters.

SHERRIED CHEESECAKE TRIFLE

Make the day before for best flavor.

750g packaged cream cheese
4 egg yolks
¾ cup castor sugar
2 teaspoons grated lemon rind
⅓ cup lemon juice
¾ cup milk
½ cup sweet sherry
375g packaged plain sweet
** biscuits**
ground nutmeg
3 x 250g punnets strawberries,
** halved**

Have cream cheese at room temperature. Beat cream cheese in large bowl with electric mixer until smooth, add egg yolks, sugar, lemon rind and lemon juice, beat until combined. Combine milk and sherry in bowl. Dip one-third of the biscuits into milk mixture, place over base of large serving dish. Spread one-third of the cream cheese mixture over biscuits, sprinkle with a little nutmeg, top with one-third of the strawberries. Repeat layering twice, cover; refrigerate overnight.

COFFEE MERINGUE ROLL WITH CHOCOLATE SAUCE

Meringue Roll is best made up to about six hours before serving.

4 egg whites
¾ cup castor sugar
1 tablespoon ground roasted
** hazelnuts**
1 tablespoon castor sugar, extra
FILLING
¾ cup thickened cream
2 teaspoons instant coffee powder
1 tablespoon Kahlua or Tia Maria
1 teaspoon vanilla
CHOCOLATE SAUCE
125g dark chocolate, melted
¼ cup icing sugar
300ml carton thickened cream
2 tablespoons Kahlua or Tia Maria
1 teaspoon vanilla

Prepare a Swiss roll tin (base measures 25cm x 30cm) by greasing, lining, greasing then dusting with cornflour; shake tin to remove excess cornflour.

Beat egg whites in small bowl with electric mixer until soft peaks form, gradually add sugar, beat until sugar is dissolved. Spread mixture evenly into Swiss roll tin.

Sprinkle meringue evenly with combined hazelnuts and extra sugar. Bake in moderate oven 10 minutes or until meringue is firm to touch. Remove from oven, turn onto sheet of grease-proof paper, remove paper carefully, cool flat to room temperature. Spread meringue with Filling, roll up carefully. Serve roll sliced, with Sauce.

Filling: Beat cream with combined coffee, Kahlua and vanilla until firm peaks form, refrigerate until required.

Chocolate Sauce: Place chocolate in bowl, stir in sifted icing sugar, cream, Kahlua and vanilla; stir until smooth.

MANGO AND PASSIONFRUIT CREAM CRUMBLE

If fresh mangoes are not available, you can substitute four x 425g cans drained, sliced mangoes.

4 mangoes, sliced
5 passionfruit
300g carton sour cream
2 eggs, lightly beaten
2 tablespoons castor sugar
2 tablespoons plain flour
CRUMBLE TOPPING
⅔ cup plain flour
⅓ cup brown sugar
⅓ cup coconut
1 teaspoon grated lemon rind
½ teaspoon ground cinnamon
90g butter

Combine mangoes and passionfruit pulp in shallow ovenproof dish. Combine sour cream, eggs, sugar and flour in bowl, beat with wooden spoon until smooth, pour over mango mixture, sprinkle with Topping. Bake in moderate oven 30 minutes or until set and golden brown. Serve warm or cold with whipped cream or icecream.

Crumble Topping: Combine flour, sugar, coconut, lemon rind and cinnamon in bowl; rub in butter.

SWEET TREATS

Crowning dinner party touch can be the luscious sweet delicacies served with coffee.

CHOCOLATE GINGER SUSHI

Light corn syrup is imported and available at delicatessens; there is no substitute for it in this recipe.

200g dark chocolate, melted
⅓ cup light corn syrup
200g white chocolate, melted
⅓ cup light corn syrup, extra
⅓ cup finely chopped glace ginger
⅓ cup finely chopped walnuts
⅓ cup finely chopped glace cherries
icing sugar

Stir corn syrup gradually into warm dark chocolate, stir constantly away from heat, until mixture thickens slightly and loses its shine. Place mixture onto piece of plastic wrap, cover well to exclude air, stand 1 hour or until chocolate is firm, but still pliable. Repeat with white chocolate and extra corn syrup. Combine ginger, walnuts and cherries in bowl. Place dark chocolate between 2 pieces of plastic wrap which have been dusted with sifted icing sugar. Roll chocolate out evenly to a 20cm square. Repeat with white chocolate.

Place dark chocolate square on top of white chocolate square, cut into 2 x 10cm squares. Place ginger mixture evenly along centre of each square, carefully roll each chocolate sheet, using the plastic wrap to form a roll. Cover, refrigerate for at least 1 hour before cutting into slices.

ALMOND TUILES

Make a day ahead if preferred: store in airtight container.

1 egg white
¼ cup castor sugar
¼ cup plain flour
½ teaspoon vanilla
2 tablespoons flaked almonds
30g butter, melted

Combine egg white in bowl with sugar, sifted flour, vanilla, almonds and butter; mix well. Place 1½ teaspoons of mixture well apart on greased oven trays to allow for spreading. For easy handling it is best to bake only 3 Tuiles at a time. Spread mixture out into circles with the back of a teaspoon. Bake in moderate oven for about 5 minutes. Remove immediately from tray with spatula, place over rolling pin to cool.

Makes about 35.

FRUIT MINCE AND APPLE TARTLETS

Tartlets can be made up to a day ahead of serving, but we prefer them served warm straight after cooking.

PASTRY
1 cup plain flour
90g butter
1 egg yolk
1 tablespoon lemon juice, approximately
FILLING
1 cup fruit mince
½ cup finely chopped walnuts
1 apple, peeled, finely chopped
1 tablespoon grated lemon rind
1 tablespoon dark rum

Pastry: Sift flour into bowl; rub in butter, add egg yolk and enough lemon juice to mix to a firm dough. Shape into a round, cover, refrigerate 30 minutes. Roll Pastry out thinly on lightly floured surface, cut into 5cm rounds, press into small fluted tartlet tins. Place a teaspoon of Filling into each case. Bake in moderate oven for about 10 minutes or until Pastry is golden brown. Dust with sifted icing sugar before serving.
Filling: Combine fruit mince, walnuts, apple, lemon rind and rum in bowl.

Makes about 24.

MINI APRICOT FLORENTINES

Make up to two weeks ahead if desired; store in airtight container in the refrigerator.

60g butter
⅓ cup brown sugar
2 tablespoons plain flour
½ cup slivered almonds, finely chopped
¼ cup finely chopped dried apricots
125g dark chocolate, melted

Cream butter and sugar in bowl until just combined, stir in sifted flour, then almonds and apricots. Drop ½ teaspoons of mixture onto lightly greased oven trays; allow room for spreading. It is best to bake only up to 6 at a time.

Bake in moderate oven for about 5 minutes or until golden brown. Remove from oven, loosen with spatula, then push each Florentine into a round shape while still hot. Lift Florentines onto wire rack to cool. Spread chocolate on flat side of each Florentine, place on foil-covered tray, run a fork through chocolate, refrigerate until chocolate is set. Store in airtight container in refrigerator.

Makes about 50.

Back: Almond Tuiles; centre, from left: Mini Apricot Florentines; Fruit Mince and Apple Tartlets; Chocolate Ginger Sushi.

MOIST COCONUT ALMOND CAKE

You will need to buy a 200g packet macaroons. Use coconut or almond-flavored macaroons. Amaretto is an almond-flavored liqueur.

¼ cup macaroon crumbs
½ cup coconut
2 tablespoons Amaretto
125g butter
½ cup castor sugar
2 eggs, separated
¼ cup macaroon crumbs, extra
¼ cup plain flour

Combine macaroon crumbs, coconut and Amaretto in bowl, press evenly over base of well-greased and base-lined deep 20cm round cake tin.

Cream butter and sugar in small bowl with electric mixer until light and fluffy. Beat in egg yolks gradually, stir in extra macaroons and sifted flour, transfer mixture to a large bowl. Beat egg whites until soft peaks form, fold gently into cake mixture, spread evenly into cake tin, bake in moderate oven for about 30 minutes. Stand 10 minutes before turning onto wire rack to cool. Serve dusted with sifted icing sugar.

RIGHT: From top: Nutty Caramel Triangles; Ginger and Lemon Bars; Rich Almond Apricot Cake.
BELOW: From left: Moist Coconut Almond Cake; Lemon Coconut and Strawberry Flan.

LEMON COCONUT AND STRAWBERRY FLAN

Flan can be cooked the day before required; cover, store at room temperature. Brush with apple jelly, decorate with strawberries up to four hours before serving. Flan can be frozen (without topping) for up to two months.

PASTRY
1 cup plain flour
2 tablespoons icing sugar
60g butter
1 egg yolk
1 tablespoon water, approximately
FILLING
90g butter
2 teaspoons grated lemon rind
½ cup castor sugar
2 eggs
2 tablespoons lemon juice
1¼ cups coconut
¼ cup apple jelly
250g punnet strawberries, halved

Pastry: Sift flour and icing sugar into bowl, rub in butter. Add egg yolk and enough water to mix to a firm dough; turn onto lightly floured surface, knead lightly until smooth, cover, refrigerate 30 minutes. Roll out on lightly floured surface large enough to line a 23cm flan tin. Spread Pastry with Filling, bake in moderately hot oven 10 minutes, reduce heat to moderate, bake further 20 minutes or until golden brown, cool to room temperature. Brush flan with half the apple jelly, top with strawberries, brush with remaining apple jelly.

Filling: Cream butter, lemon rind and sugar in bowl with electric mixer, until light and fluffy; beat in eggs one at a time. Mixture might curdle slightly at this stage, but will reconstitute when coconut is added. Stir in lemon juice and coconut. Soften apple jelly over low heat.

NUTTY CARAMEL TRIANGLES

Corn syrup can be bought from health food stores or the gourmet section of your supermarket. Triangles can be wrapped and frozen for up to six months. Thaw at room temperature when required.

PASTRY
¾ cup plain flour
¾ cup self-raising flour
1 tablespoon icing sugar
125g butter
1 tablespoon water, approximately
FILLING
½ cup pecan nuts
⅓ cup blanched almonds
⅓ cup unsalted roasted cashews
1 cup light corn syrup
½ cup brown sugar
1 tablespoon plain flour
2 eggs, lightly beaten
15g butter, melted

Pastry: Sift flours and icing sugar into bowl, rub in butter, add enough water to mix to a firm dough. Knead lightly until smooth, cover, refrigerate 30 minutes. Roll dough out on lightly floured surface large enough to line base and sides of a Swiss roll tin (base measures 25cm x 30cm). Place a piece of greaseproof paper over Pastry, sprinkle thickly with dry beans or rice, bake in moderately hot oven 7 minutes. Remove beans and paper, bake further 7 minutes or until golden brown.

Sprinkle Pastry with nuts, spoon remaining ingredients over nuts. Bake in moderate oven 20 minutes or until golden brown, cool in tin.

Filling: Chop nuts coarsely (do not use blender or processor). Combine corn syrup, brown sugar, flour, eggs and butter in bowl, beat with fork.

GINGER AND LEMON BARS

We like to eat this cake within two days of cooking.

1¾ cups plain flour
1 cup castor sugar
125g glace ginger, chopped
185g butter, melted
1 egg, lightly beaten
2 tablespoons lemon juice
⅔ cup (60g) flaked almonds

Sift flour and sugar into bowl, mix in ginger, cooled butter, egg and lemon juice. Press mixture evenly over base of well-greased lamington tin (base measures 16cm x 26cm), press almonds on top. Bake in moderate oven for about 45 minutes or until golden brown, cool in tin, cut when cold.

RICH ALMOND APRICOT CAKE

This cake will keep for several months stored in an airtight container.

2 cups (250g) slivered almonds
1 cup (185g) chopped glace apricots
⅔ cup plain flour
2 tablespoons cocoa
1 teaspoon cinnamon
60g dark chocolate, melted
½ cup honey
⅓ cup sugar
icing sugar

Grease a deep 20cm round cake tin, line base and side with non-stick baking paper. Toast almonds on oven tray in moderate oven for about 5 minutes. Combine almonds, apricots, and sifted flour, cocoa and cinnamon in bowl.

Combine honey and sugar in pan, stir over low heat until sugar is dissolved, bring to the boil, reduce heat. Simmer uncovered, without stirring, for about 5 minutes or until syrup forms a soft ball when a teaspoon of the syrup is dropped into a cup of cold water.

Stir chocolate and hot syrup into almond mixture; mix well. Spread mixture evenly over base of tin, bake in slow oven for about 35 minutes (the cake will still feel a little soft at this stage). Cool in tin. Turn cake out of tin, remove paper, wrap cake in plastic food wrap, then foil. Stand at least a day before cutting.

Dust with sifted icing sugar before cutting into thin slices to serve.

PECAN ROLL WITH RASPBERRY LIQUEUR CREAM

Framboise is a raspberry-flavored li-queur. Make and assemble roll one day ahead if preferred; keep covered and refrigerated.

5 eggs, separated
¾ cup castor sugar
1¾ cups (185g) pecan nuts
¼ cup castor sugar, extra
300ml carton thickened cream
1 tablespoon Framboise
1 tablespoon icing sugar

Beat egg yolks and sugar in small bowl with electric mixer until pale and thick. Blend or process pecans until finely ground, transfer to large bowl; fold in egg yolk mixture. Beat egg whites until soft peaks form, fold gently into pecan mixture. Pour into greased and lined Swiss roll tin (base measures 25cm x 30cm), bake in moderate oven for about 20 minutes. Turn roll onto sheet of greaseproof paper dusted with ex-tra castor sugar. Remove lining paper. Roll up gently with paper; stand 1 min-ute, unroll, cool to room temperature.

Beat combined cream, liqueur and sifted icing sugar until soft peaks form. Spread three-quarters of the cream over roll, roll up carefully from the short side, place onto serving plate, decor-ate with remaining cream, extra pecan nuts and raspberries if desired.

CHOCOLATE MOUSSE ROLL WITH APRICOT CREAM

Roll is best made the day before re-quired; keep covered and refrigerated. This cake does not contain flour and will deflate when removed from the oven. Decorate just before serving. To make quick chocolate curls, shave chocolate with a vegetable peeler.

125g dark chocolate, melted
1 tablespoon instant coffee powder
2 tablespoons hot water
4 eggs, separated
¾ cup castor sugar
cocoa
APRICOT CREAM
⅓ cup chopped dried apricots
¾ cup water
1 teaspoon grated lemon rind
2 tablespoons sugar
1 tablespoon Grand Marnier
1 teaspoon lemon juice
300ml carton thickened cream

Stir combined coffee and water into chocolate. Beat egg yolks and sugar in small bowl with electric mixer until thick and pale. Transfer mixture to large bowl, stir in cooled chocolate mixture. Beat egg whites until soft peaks form, fold into mixture. Pour into greased and lined Swiss roll tin (base measures 25cm x 30cm), bake in mod-erate oven 10 minutes or until springy to touch. Leave cake in tin, cover with a well wrung-out damp cloth for about 2 hours. Turn cake onto greaseproof paper which has been dusted with sift-ed cocoa. Spread cake evenly with Apricot Cream, roll up gently from the short side. Place onto serving dish, decorate with extra whipped cream, apricots and grated chocolate.

Apricot Cream: Place apricots and water in pan, bring to the boil; reduce heat, simmer, covered, for 10 minutes or until apricots are just tender. Add lemon rind and sugar, simmer further 5 minutes. Add Grand Marnier and lemon juice, blend or process until smooth, cool; refrigerate 30 minutes. Beat cream until soft peaks form, fold into apricot mixture.

CHOCOLATE RAINBOW MERINGUES

This recipe will make about 60 small Meringues. The amount of chocolate specified is enough for 20. We suggest you use the rest of the Meringue mixture to make larger Meringues or a Pavlova. The chocolate-dipped Meringues can be made two days before required; keep refrigerated.

1 egg white
⅓ cup castor sugar
1 teaspoon instant coffee powder
1 teaspoon hot water
1 teaspoon lemon juice
150g milk chocolate, chopped
2 tablespoons oil
100g dark chocolate, chopped

LEFT: From top: Chocolate Rainbow Meringues; Mini Apple Tarte Tatin.
BELOW: From left: Pecan Roll with Raspberry Liqueur Cream; Chocolate Mousse Roll with Apricot Cream.

Beat egg white in small bowl with electric mixer until soft peaks form, gradually add sugar, beating well after each addition; beat until sugar is dissolved. Add combined coffee and hot water and lemon juice. Place Meringue into a piping bag fitted with a plain 1cm tube. Pipe smooth, flat 2cm rounds of Meringue onto oven trays covered with non-stick baking paper or foil.

Bake in very slow oven for about 30 minutes or until Meringues are firm to the touch. Leave door ajar, allow Meringues to cool in oven.

Melt milk chocolate in bowl over hot water (or microwave on HIGH 2 minutes), stir in 1 tablespoon of the oil. Dip two-thirds of each Meringue into the milk chocolate, place onto foil-covered tray, refrigerate until set. Melt dark chocolate, add remaining oil. Dip each Meringue into dark chocolate, to cover half the milk chocolate; return to tray, refrigerate until set.

Makes 20.

MINI APPLE TARTE TATIN

Serve warm or cold; make the same day as serving.

2 sheets ready-rolled puff pastry
4 apples, peeled
¼ cup castor sugar
½ cup apricot jam

Place the pastry sheets on top of each other, cut into 3 equal lengths. Place pastry pieces onto oven tray, slightly apart; top evenly with thinly sliced apples, sprinkle evenly with sugar. Bake in very hot oven 20 minutes, reduce heat to moderate, bake further 10 minutes or until golden brown. Melt apricot jam gently in pan (or microwave on HIGH for about 1 minute). Brush jam all over apples. Cut into squares to serve.

Makes about 30

PORT AND PRUNE TRUFFLES

Truffles will keep in refrigerator, covered, for several weeks.

½ cup finely chopped prunes
¼ cup port
1½ cups cake crumbs, lightly packed
¼ cup slivered almonds, finely chopped
¼ cup cream
¼ teaspoon almond essence
2 tablespoons oil
250g dark chocolate, melted

Combine prunes and port in pan, bring to the boil, reduce heat, simmer uncovered, few minutes, or until all the liquid is absorbed. Combine prunes, cake crumbs, almonds, cream and almond essence together in bowl; mix well, refrigerate several hours or until firm. Shape teaspoons of mixture into balls, place on tray, refrigerate 1 hour. Add oil to chocolate, dip balls into chocolate mixture, place onto foil-covered tray; refrigerate until set.

Makes about 40.

TWO-CHOCOLATE TRUFFLES

Truffles will keep in refrigerator, covered, for several weeks. Use any plain cake for the cake crumbs, blend or process cake until fine.

2 cups cake crumbs, lightly packed
2 teaspoons grated orange rind
2 tablespoons Cointreau
100g dark chocolate, melted
¼ cup cream
2 tablespoons oil
250g white chocolate, melted

Combine cake crumbs, orange rind, Cointreau, dark chocolate and cream in bowl; mix well. Refrigerate mixture for several hours, or until firm. Shape teaspoons of mixture into balls, place in single layer on tray, cover, refrigerate 1 hour. Stir oil into white chocolate, dip balls into chocolate, place onto foil-covered tray; refrigerate until set.

Makes about 45.

CHOC-HAZELNUT PINWHEELS

Marzipan rolls and Nutella (chocolate hazelnut spread) are available from supermarkets and delicatessens.

200g marzipan roll
icing sugar
¼ cup Nutella
200g dark chocolate, melted

Roll marzipan to 22cm x 30cm rectangle on surface dusted lightly with sifted icing sugar. Spread evenly all over with Nutella, roll up like a Swiss roll from the long side, cover, refrigerate for several hours or until firm. Spread with chocolate, place on foil-covered tray; refrigerate until set. Cut roll into thin slices to serve.

APRICOT AND CASHEW CHOCOLATE CLUSTERS

Clusters will keep for up to two weeks, covered, in refrigerator.

⅔ cup (100g) chopped glace apricots
¼ cup dry white wine
125g packet cream cheese
¾ cup (150g) unsalted roasted cashews, chopped
1 teaspoon vanilla
2 tablespoons icing sugar, sifted
⅓ cup coconut
250g white chocolate, chopped
2 tablespoons oil
250g dark chocolate, chopped
2 tablespoons oil, extra

Combine apricots and wine in bowl, cover, stand 1 hour; drain. Have cream cheese at room temperature. Beat cream cheese until smooth, stir in apricots, cashews, vanilla, icing sugar and coconut. Drop teaspoonfuls of mixture onto foil-covered trays, refrigerate several hours or until firm.

Melt 200g of the white chocolate with oil over hot water (or microwave on HIGH for about 2 minutes). Melt 200g of the dark chocolate with extra oil the same way. Coat half the Clusters in white chocolate and remaining Clusters in dark chocolate, place onto foil-covered trays, refrigerate until set. Melt remaining white and dark chocolate separately. Pipe or drizzle thin lines of chocolate over the Clusters; refrigerate until set.

Makes about 50.

CHOCOLATE COCONUT ICE

There is no substitute for liquid glucose in this recipe. Coconut Ice can be made several weeks ahead; keep covered in refrigerator.

4 cups sugar
1 cup milk
2 tablespoons liquid glucose
2¾ cups (250g) coconut
125g dark chocolate, melted

Combine sugar, milk and glucose in pan, stir over heat without boiling until sugar is dissolved. Bring to the boil, boil steadily without stirring until temperature reaches 112°C on a sweets thermometer, or until a teaspoon of syrup forms a soft ball when dropped into a cup of cold water.

Remove from heat, divide mixture into two bowls, divide coconut between bowls. Stir mixture in 1 bowl with a wooden spoon until thick and creamy, press evenly over base of greased and lined 23cm square slab tin. Stir chocolate into remaining coconut mixture, beat until thick and creamy. Spread chocolate mixture over white mixture. Refrigerate until firm before cutting.

CARAMEL WALNUT GATEAU

Cake can be made and layered with Filling the day before required, keep covered and refrigerated. Decorate just before serving.

3 eggs
½ cup castor sugar
1 tablespoon caramel topping
1 cup (100g) walnut pieces
½ cup self raising flour
¼ cup boiling water
2 teaspoons butter
300ml carton thickened cream
CARAMEL FILLING
¼ cup brown sugar
30g butter
2 tablespoons custard powder
¼ cup milk
300ml carton cream
PRALINE
½ cup sugar
⅓ cup walnuts

Beat eggs in small bowl with electric mixer until pale and thick, gradually add sugar and topping, beat for about 10 minutes or until sugar is dissolved; transfer mixture to large bowl. Blend or process walnuts until finely ground, fold into egg mixture, lightly fold in sifted flour, then combined water and butter. Pour mixture into 2 greased and base-lined 20 cm sandwich tins. Bake in moderate oven 20 minutes, turn onto wire rack to cool. Split each cake in half horizontally.

Place 1 layer of cake onto serving plate, spread with one-third of the Filling. Repeat layering with Filling and cake. Cover, refrigerate several hours.

Whip cream until soft peaks form, spread over top and side of cake. Press Praline around side of cake. Decorate with extra cream, walnuts and fruit, if desired.

Caramel Filling: Combine sugar and butter in pan, stir over low heat until sugar is dissolved, stir in blended custard powder and milk, then cream. Stir constantly over heat until mixture boils and thickens; cool.

Praline: Place sugar in heavy pan over medium heat until sugar begins to melt; do not stir, When sugar starts to brown, stir gently to dissolve remaining sugar. Spread walnuts onto lightly greased oven tray, pour hot syrup evenly over walnuts. When set, break into pieces, blend or process until ground finely.

LEFT: Top: Port and Prune Truffles and Two-Chocolate Truffles; centre: Choc-Hazelnut Pinwheels; bottom, from left: Chocolate Coconut Ice; Apricot and Cashew Chocolate Clusters.

MOIST APPLE AND HAZELNUT CAKE

Calvados is an apple-flavored brandy; ordinary brandy can be used as a substitute if preferred

3 eggs, separated
½ cup castor sugar
1 cup (125g) roasted hazelnuts
1 apple, peeled, grated
300ml carton thickened cream
1 tablespoon Calvados
1 tablespoon icing sugar

Beat egg yolks and sugar in small bowl with electric mixer until pale and thick; transfer to large bowl. Blend or process hazelnuts until finely chopped, fold into egg mixture with apple. Beat egg whites until soft peaks form, fold gently into hazelnut mixture. Pour into greased and lined 20cm springform pan, bake in moderate oven 30 minutes. Remove springform side, stand cake until it is cold. Turn cake onto serving plate. Beat cream with Calvados and sifted icing sugar until soft peaks form. Spread top and side of cake with whipped cream. Decorate with grated chocolate if desired.

LAYERED ORANGE SPONGE

Cake can be frozen for up to one month. Assemble with cream on same day as serving.

4 eggs
2 teaspoons grated orange rind
⅔ cup castor sugar
1 cup self raising flour
15g butter
2 tablespoons boiling water
2 x 300ml cartons thickened cream
2 tablespoons Grand Marnier
2 tablespoons icing sugar

Beat eggs, orange rind and sugar in small bowl with electric mixer until pale and thick. Transfer mixture to large bowl. Gently fold in sifted flour, then combined butter and water. Pour mixture into greased and lined Swiss roll tin (base measures 25cm x 30cm), bake in moderate oven 25 minutes, turn onto wire rack to cool. Cut cake into 3 pieces. Whip combined cream, Grand Marnier and sifted icing sugar until soft peaks form. Place 1 layer of cake onto serving plate, spread with some of the cream, continue layering with cake and cream.

Cover top and sides of cake with remaining cream. Decorate with thin strips of orange rind and orange segments if desired.

HAZELNUT MERINGUE CAKE WITH KAHLUA CREAM

Cake will cut better if made the day before required; cover and refrigerate.

1 cup (125g) ground roasted hazelnuts
4 egg whites
1 cup castor sugar
1 teaspoon vanilla
1 teaspoon white vinegar
200g dark chocolate, chopped
60g butter
KAHLUA CREAM
125g packet cream cheese
60g butter
⅓ cup castor sugar
¼ cup Kahlua or Tia Maria
300ml carton thickened cream

Toast hazelnuts on oven tray in moderate oven for about 5 minutes; cool. Beat egg whites in small bowl with electric mixer until soft peaks form. Gradually add sugar, beating well after each addition; beat until sugar is dissolved. Fold in vanilla, vinegar and hazelnuts. Spread into 2 x 23cm circles on 2 oven trays covered with non-stick baking paper, bake in moderate oven 25 minutes or until firm; cool.

Melt chocolate and butter in bowl over hot water (or microwave on HIGH 2 minutes), spread evenly over meringue layers. Spread with half the Cream. Top with other meringue layer, chocolate side down. Spread top and side of cake with remaining Cream, decorate with strawberries and extra whipped cream if desired.

Kahlua Cream: Have cream cheese and butter at room temperature. Beat cream cheese, butter and sugar in small bowl with electric mixer until light and fluffy, add Kahula and cream, beat until combined.

LEFT: From top: Moist Apple and Hazelnut Cake; Caramel Walnut Gateau; Layered Orange Sponge.
RIGHT: Hazelnut Meringue Cake with Kahlua Cream.

GLOSSARY

Some terms, names and alternatives are included here to help everyone use our recipes perfectly.

Arrowroot: a thickening ingredient; cornflour can be substituted.

Beef eye fillet: tenderloin.

Bicarbonate of soda: baking soda.

Breadcrumbs:

Dry: use commercially packaged breadcrumbs.

Stale: use 1 or 2 day old white or wholemeal bread made into crumbs by grating, blending or processing.

Buttermilk: the liquid left from separated cream, slightly sour in taste; use skim milk if unavailable.

Cannellini beans: small white beans.

Caramel topping: a flavoring used in milk drinks or on icecream sundaes.

Cheese: tasty: cheddar cheese.

Chicken Maryland: a chicken piece consisting of the joined leg (drumstick) and thigh.

Chilli:

Fresh: use rubber gloves when handling these hot vegetables. Use ½ teaspoon chilli powder instead of 1 medium chilli, if preferred.

Powder: we used the hot Asian variety.

Sauce: we used the hot Asian variety except where sweet chilli sauce is specified.

Chocolate:

Dark: we used a good quality cooking chocolate.

Milk: we used a light chocolate bar.

White: we used a white chocolate bar.

Coconut milk: available in supermarkets in cans or cartons.

Cooking salt: a coarse salt (not fine table salt).

Cornflour: cornstarch

Corn syrup: an imported product available at delicatessens.

Cream:

Pouring: light cream or half 'n' half.

Thickened: whipping or double cream.

Sour: a thick commercially cultured soured cream.

Light sour: a less dense commercially cultured soured cream.

Custard powder: pudding mix.

Dried yeast: 3 level teaspoons dried yeast is equivalent to 30g compressed yeast. Dissolve in fairly hot water.

Eggplant: aubergine.

Essence: extract.

Five spice powder: a mixture of ground spices which includes cinnamon, cloves, fennel, star anise and Szechwan pepper.

Flour:

Plain: all-purpose flour.

Self-raising flour: substitute plain (all-purpose) flour and baking powder in the proportion of ¾ metric cup plain flour to 2 level metric teaspoons baking powder. Sift together several times before using. If using an 8oz measuring cup, use 1 cup plain flour to 2 teaspoons baking powder.

Fresh ginger: ginger root.

Fruit mince: mincemeat.

Green ginger wine: an Australian-made alcoholic sweet wine infused with finely ground ginger.

Golden syrup, treacle: maple/pancake syrup. Substitute honey.

Green shallots: scallions or spring onions in some Australian states.

Grill/griller: broil/broiler.

Herbs:

Dried leaves: use dehydrated leaf of herb. When fresh herbs are specified but unavailable, use ¼ of the dried leaf variety instead of the fresh; e.g. use 1 teaspoon dried basil leaves as a substitute for 1 tablespoon (4 teaspoons) chopped fresh basil. This is not recommended when more than a tablespoon of fresh herbs is to be substituted.

Ground: use powdered form (also spices).

Hoisin sauce: is a thick sweet Chinese barbecue sauce made from salted black beans, onions and garlic.

Kiwi fruit: Chinese gooseberry.

Liquid glucose: (glucose syrup) made from wheat starch; available at health food stores and supermarkets.

Lamington tin: a rectangular slab tin with a depth of 4cm.

Minced beef: ground beef.

Mixed spice: a finely ground combination of spices which include caraway, allspice, coriander, cumin, nutmeg, ginger and cinnamon; almost always used in sweet recipes.

Pawpaw: papaya.

Peppers: (capsicums) sweet or bell peppers, red or green.

Pimentos: sweet red peppers preserved in brine in cans or jars.

Punnet: basket holding 250g fruit.

Rockmelon: cantaloupe.

Sambal oelak: a paste made from ground chillies and salt.

Snow peas: also known as mangetout, sugar peas or Chinese peas, are small flat pods with barely formed peas; they are eaten whole. Top, tail and string snow peas. Cook for a short time (about 30 seconds) either by stirfrying or blanching.

Soy sauce: is made form fermented soy beans. The light sauce is generally used with white meat dishes, and the darker variety with red meat dishes. The dark soy is generally used for color and the light for flavor. We used Soy Superior, the dark variety, and Superior Soy, the light variety.

Spinach: we have used the flat leafed English spinach, or the darker spinach, also known as silver beet.

Spring onions: vegetables with small white bulbs and long green leaves.

Stock: we used fish, chicken or beef stock in this book, stock cubes can be used in the proportion of 1 small stock cube to 1 cup water.

Sugar:

Castor: use regular granulated table or berry sugar.

Icing: confectioners' or powdered sugar. We used icing sugar mixture.

Sultanas: seedless white raisins.

Sweet biscuits: any plain sweet biscuit (or cookie) can be used.

Taco seasoning mix, Taco shells: both are available in supermarkets amongst Mexican ingredients.

Zucchini: courgette.

Cup and Spoon Measurements

To ensure accuracy in your recipes use the standard metric measuring equipment approved by Standards Australia:

(a) 250 millilitre cup for measuring liquids. A litre jug (capacity 4 cups) is also available.

(b) a graduated set of four cups – measuring 1 cup, half, third and quarter cup – for items such as flour, sugar, etc. When measuring in these fractional cups, level of at the brim.

(c) a graduated set of four spoons – tablespoon (20 millilitre liquid capacity), teaspoon (5 millilitre), half and quarter teaspoons. The Australian, British and American teaspoon each has 5m capacity.

Approximate cup and spoon conversion chart

Australian	American & British
1 cup	1¼ cups
¾ cup	1 cup
⅔ cup	¾ cup
½ cup	⅔ cup
⅓ cup	½ cup
¼ cup	⅓ cup
2 tablespoons	¼ cup
1 tablespoon	3 teaspoons

All spoon measurements are level.

Note: NZ, USA and UK all use 15ml tablespoons.

We have used large eggs with an average weight of 60g each in all recipes.

OVEN TEMPERATURES

Electric	C°	F°
Very slow	120	250
Slow	150	300
Moderately slow	160-180	325-350
Moderate	180-200	375-400
Moderately hot	210-230	425-450
Hot	240-250	475-500
Very hot	260	525-550

Gas	C°	F°
Very slow	120	250
Slow	150	300
Moderately slow	160	325
Moderate	180	350
Moderately hot	190	375
Hot	200	400
Very hot	230	450

INDEX

ACKNOWLEDGMENTS

We would like to thank the following for providing photographic props:
Artiana Imports, Sydney — glassware; Barbeques Galore — barbecues; Dansab Pty. Ltd., Sydney — china; David Jones, Sydney — furniture; Fitz & Floyd (Kosta Boda Australia) — china and glassware; Formica — laminate; Fred Pazotti Pty. Ltd. — tiles; Hale Imports — china; House of Bambusit, Sydney — table and chair; Jaan, Sydney — fabric; KWL Imports, Sydney — glassware; Lifestyle Imports, Sydney — china; Mikasa Tableware (NSW) Pty. Ltd. — china; Metro Marble — marble; Net Sales, Sydney — fishing nets; Novo Industries — plastic picnic utensils; Orrefors, Australia, Pty. Ltd. — glassware; Robert Green, Sydney — fabric, table linen; Royal Doulton — china; Scanada Agencies and Imports — wooden board; Statements, Sydney — china and gift items; Studio Haus, Sydney — china, table linen, glassware; The Flower Man, Double Bay, NSW — flowers, plants; Ukiyo-no, Annandale, NSW — Japanese furniture; Vasa Agencies (Australia) Pty. Ltd. — plastic utensils, cutlery, kitchenware; Villa Italiana, Sydney — Italian ceramic china; Villeroy & Boch (Australia) Pty. Ltd. — china; Wedgwood Australia Ltd. — china; Wilson Fabrics, Sydney — fabric.